Aliaksandr Sukhanevich

The Japanese Light Cruiser Ōyodo

KAGERO

Starboard side view.

Project

According to the Japanese concept of submarine warfare, Imperial Navy's submarines were to operate over a large area and attack enemy fleet. To coordinate their activities and search for targets surface flagships were needed. Occasionally used in such role old 5,500-ton cruisers did not meet the requirements of the Japanese command. Therefore, new flagships were needed for each of the seven flotillas. The requirements for these cruisers concerned a long range of operation, high speed, strong armament in the event of encountering light enemy units, reconnaissance aircraft, as well as appropriate means of communication and rooms for staff personnel. Of the many variants prepared by the technical service, the design of the C-type cruiser, completed in October 1938, was selected. The increase in autonomy came at the expense of armour. It was the first such case in the Japanese fleet. Originally it was planned to arm the cruiser with four 152.4 mm/50 guns (similar to the Agano class light cruisers), but the ship's dimensions allowed for the deployment of two 155-mm/60 gun turrets, removed from heavy cruisers of the Mogami class. The cruiser was to receive new E15K1 hydroplanes designed to perform reconnaissance tasks in areas where the enemy had the air superiority.

The plan assumed to build two such ships as part of the fourth program 1937/38. The funds for the construction of two flagships for the submarine flotilla were granted in March 1938. As the design by Commander Fukuda did not fully satisfy the command (too small range), the fifth fleet replenishment program included the construction of five more cruisers numbered 810–814. In year 1945 they became the "standard" light cruisers of the Japanese fleet.

Table No. 1. Dates of construction of the Ōyodo type ships

Name	Shipyard	Number	Dates			Fate
			Keel	Launch	Finish	
"Ōyodo"	Navy Shipyard in Kure	136	February 14, 1941	April 2, 1942	February 28, 1943	Sank on July 28, 1945
"Niyodo"	Navy Shipyard in Kure	137	–	–	–	Order cancelled

Construction

The hull of the new cruiser, borrowed from the previous Agano type, had a smooth deck, slightly raised in the fore part with a bow bulb, which reduced water resistance. Navigation devices and artillery fire control posts were placed on the turret-like bow superstructure. In the aft part there was an airtight hangar (with forced ventilation) and a catapult.

The cruiser's main armament consisted of six 155 mm/60 Type 3 guns housed in two triple turrets on the foredeck. The turrets were dismantled from Mogami class cruisers when they were rearmed with 203 mm artillery. The fire unit consisted of 140 rounds per barrel. The long-range AA artillery consisted of eight 100 mm/65 Type 98 rapid-firing guns in four twin mounts, two on each side of amidships. The same guns were carried by Akizuki class destroyers and were considered by the Japanese to be their best heavy anti-aircraft guns. Fire unit

Port side view.

consisted of 310 unitary rounds. The short-range AA defence originally consisted of six 25 mm/60 Type 96 guns in two triple mounts. Fire unit – 2200 unitary rounds. "Ōyodo" was the only Japanese light cruiser without torpedo tubes. Two searchlights with a mirror diameter of 110 cm were used to illuminate the targets at night.

The entire aft deck of the cruiser was intended for air operations. The cruiser could carry six reconnaissance floatplanes Type 2 – Kawanishi E15K1 *Shiun* ("Purple Cloud") on board (the Allies gave it the code name "Norm"). Four machines were stored in hangar and the other two on the open deck. Because the seaplane turned out to be almost a ton heavier than its predecessor E13A1, a special 45-meter catapult Type 2 No. 1 mod. 10 was designed for its launch (working length 35 m, permissible weight of the aircraft up to 5000 kg). The E15K1 disappointed the expectations. It turned out to be much slower than planned (468 km/h). To make matters worse, its production caused problems: only 15 copies of this machine were produced, 6 of which went to the "Ōyodo", but they were shot down very quickly.

The main artillery fire control system included the Type 94 computer and one 8-meter rangefinder (on the tower No. 2), and one 6-meter (on the bridge). The 100-mm AA artillery was equipped with two calculators with two 4.5-meter Type 94 rangefinders. The control of anti-aircraft fire was performed by three Type 95 computers.

Passive protection was designed to protect the ship against the impact of 152-mm shells or a 250 kg bomb dropped from a height of 3,000 m. The main armour belt, 50 mm thick, was attached to the outer plating, it was 71 m long and 3.91 m high. In the ammunition chambers area, it smoothly changed into an internal one with a thickness of 40 to 75 mm. The length of this section was 35 meters, and the height of the armour plates – 2.6 m. Together with the bow and stern 50 mm thick traverses, it formed an armoured citadel protecting the bow ammunition chambers, boiler and machine compartments amidships. The armour thickness of the main deck was 28–30 mm above the engine room and 50 mm above the ammunition chambers. Turret barbets: No. 1 – 20 mm, No. 2 – 30 mm. Main artillery turret armour: 25.4 – 10 – 5.4 mm; ammunition chambers of 155-mm guns: 75 mm (upper belt), 40 mm (lower belt); command post: 40–20–20 mm. The total armour weight was 987 tons (about 9.5% of the cruiser displacement).

The cruiser was powered by four sets of Kampon steam turbines with a total power of 110,000 HP. The steam was produced by 6 Kampon "RO GO" water-tube boilers (pressure: 30 kg/cm^2, temperature: 350°C), fired with fuel oil. Each set of turbines developed 27,500 hp at 340 rpm forward and 6,875 hp at 147 rpm reverse power. Each set of turbines consisted of three front turbines (high, medium and low pressure) geared onto one shaft by a three-tooth helical gear. Each of the embankments ended with a 3-blade propeller 3.50 m in diameter. The maximum speed was 35 knots, and the economy was 14 knots. In full power turbine tests on February 19, 1943, the "Ōyodo" achieved a top speed of 35.50 knots with 111,220 hp at 339.4 rpm (displacement 10,467 t). The maximum capacity of the fuel tanks was 2,445 t with an expected swimming range of 8,700 nautical miles at a speed of 18 knots. The actual swimming range turned out to be much larger – 10,315 nautical miles.

Modifications

The first modification of the "Ōyodo" was made in April 1943. A Type 21 radar was then installed on the rangefinder turret. Another modification (March 6–23, 1944 in Yokosuka) was connected with the change of the role of the cruiser, which became the flagship of the Combined Fleet. As a result, the aircraft hangar was rebuilt to accommodate conference rooms and quarters for staff personnel. The large catapult was replaced with a smaller standard one, 18.9 m long. The number of seaplanes was reduced to two. The number of anti-aircraft guns was increased by adding six triple mounts and eleven single ones. The ship now carried a total of 47 25-mm guns. Radars were also installed: one Type 13 (on the mast above the hangar) and two Type 22 (on the side platforms of the bow superstructure). Ship boats have been reduced to four. In October 1944, 10 25-mm guns were added in two stages – first six singles, and then, at the end of the month, four more. The final number of 25-mm artillery increased to 57 barrels (12 × 3 and 21 × 1).

War service

After entering the service, until April 1943, she underwent training in the Inner Sea. On April 1 this year, she was included to the 8th Cruiser Squadron of the 3rd Fleet (aircraft carriers). In July, she moved troops from Japan to Rabaul, New Britain. Ship spent the next seven months on the Truk Atoll. On December 6, she became the flagship of the 3rd Fleet. In the period from December 30, 1943 to January 1, 1944, she transported troops to Kavieng in New Ireland.

On January 1, it was attacked by American planes, but only slightly damaged. In February, she made a transport cruise to Saipan and returned to Japan in March 1944. After renovation and modernization at Yokosuka, from April 30, 1944, she served as the flagship of the Joint Fleet.

On October 20, 1944, she embarked as an escort of aircraft carriers to take part in the Battle of Leyte Bay. During the battle near Cape Engano on October 25, the cruiser sustained minor damage as a result of direct hits from one bomb and two rockets. Eight people perished and 12 were injured. After damage inflicted to the aircraft carrier "Zuikaku", Vice Admiral Ozawa raised his flag on the "Ōyodo". On November 15 she was included to the 2nd Fleet.

On December 26–28, "Ōyodo" took part in the rally to the American beachhead near San Jose (Mindoro Island, Philippines). Operating on December 27, 1944, she was hit by two 250-kg bombs dropped from US planes. On January 1, 1945, the ship was included in the 5th Squadron of the Southwestern Fleet. From January 9 to 29 she underwent the refurbishment in Singapore. From February 10, 1945, it was part of the 4th Aircraft Carrier Division.

In February 1945, "Ōyodo" was ordered to ferry to Japan. The cruiser left Singapore with the battleships "Ise" and "Hyuga" with a load of rubber, aviation gasoline, tin and other metals. During the voyage, Japanese ships were repeatedly attacked by American submarines. One torpedo hit "Ōyodo" (damage size unknown), but remained buoyant. On February 20, 1945, the group arrived safely in Japan.

On March 1, 1945, "Ōyodo" joined the School Complex in Kure. During the US air raid on Kure on March 19, three bombs hit "Ōyodo", severely damaging the engine-room compartments. Fifty four people died. Renovated in Kure, she returned to service. During another US air raid on Kure on July 24, the cruiser was hit by five bombs, in addition, four more exploded nearby. The damage to the ship turned out to be very serious, a heavy fire broke out, which was put out only after two days. July 28 was critical for the cruiser, when it received four direct bomb hits during the air raid. As a result, it settled to the bottom with a strong inclination to the port side. About 300 people died. "Ōyodo" was removed from the fleet list on November 20, 1945. In 1947 the ship was raised and in 1948 scrapped.

Tactical and technical data of the cruiser "Ōyodo" (February 1943)

Displacement: std 8,534 t; full 11,433 t (9,980 t design; 10,417 t on trials);
Dimensions: 180/189.7 (water line) / 192 × 16.6 × 5.95 (6.1) m;
Power plant: 4 Kampon turbines, 6 KP Kampon; 110,000 hp; 2,445 tons of heating oil;
Speed: 35 knots; range 10315 Mm/18 knots;
Armour: sides 40–75 mm, deck 28–50 mm, turrets 25 mm;
Weapons: 2 × 3 – 155 mm/60, 4 × 2 – 100 mm/65, 6 × 3 – 25 mm/60, 2 depth charges launchers (6 depth charges), 1 catapult, 6 seaplanes;
Crew: 786 men (including 53 officers).

Table No. 2. Technical data of the artillery of the cruiser "Ōyodo"

	15.5 cm	10 cm	2.5 cm
Station model	1	Mod.1 mod. A	1
Type	3	98	95
Caliber, mm	155	100	25
Barrel length, in calibers	60	65	60
Barrel elevation angle, degrees	+55	+90	+80
Gun weight with the breech, kg	12700	3053	115
Mass of the rotating part of the station or turret, tons	175 177,1 for mod. 2	20.4	0.785 (for 1 × 1) 1.1 (for 1 × 2) 1.8 (for 1 × 3)
Rate of fire, rounds per minute	5–7	15	110–200
Range, m/barrel elevation angle	25 000/35	19 500/•	7500/•
Ceiling, m/barrel elevation angle	•	13 000/90	5500/85

Table No. 3. Technical data of seaplanes

	E15K1	E13A1
Type	2	0 mod. 1
Year of production	1942–1944	1940–1945
Dimensions, m	14.0 × 11,6 × 4.95	14.5 × 11.27 × 4.78
Number of engines × power in hp	1 × 1620	1 × 1080
Take-off weight, kg	4900	4000
Top speed, km/h	468	370
Cruising speed, km/h	296	222
Ceiling, m	11 400	14 960
Range, km	3370	3320
Armament: number × calibre in mm	1 × 7,7/1 bomb 120 kg	1 × 20, 2 × 7,7/1 bomb 250 kg or 4 bombs 60 kg each
Crew	2	3

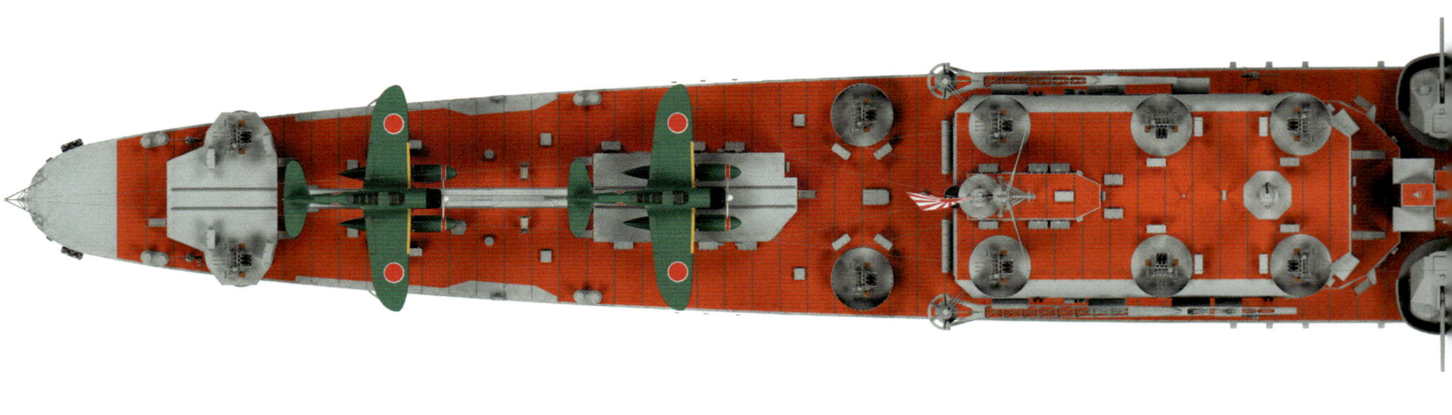

Bow view.

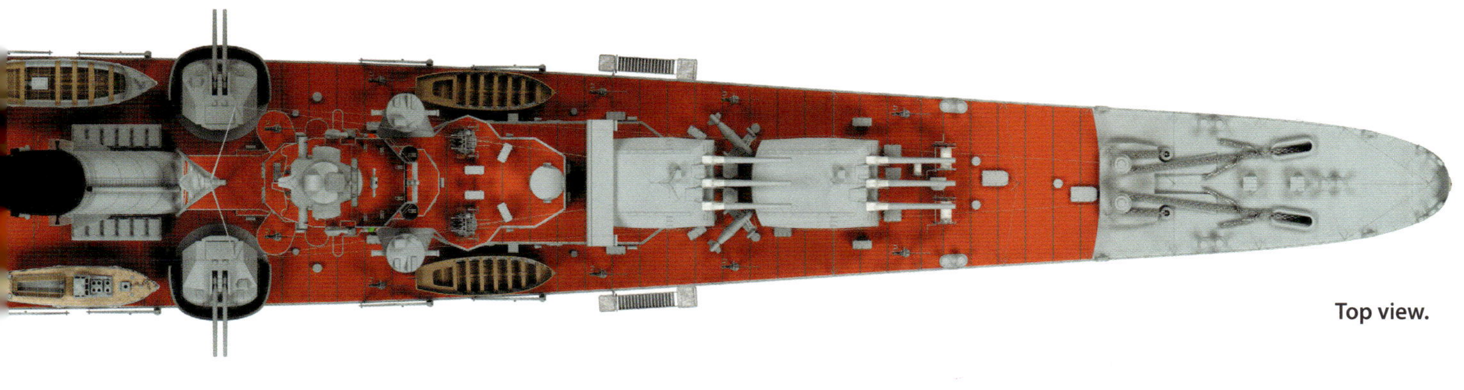

Top view.

Bow view.

Stern view.

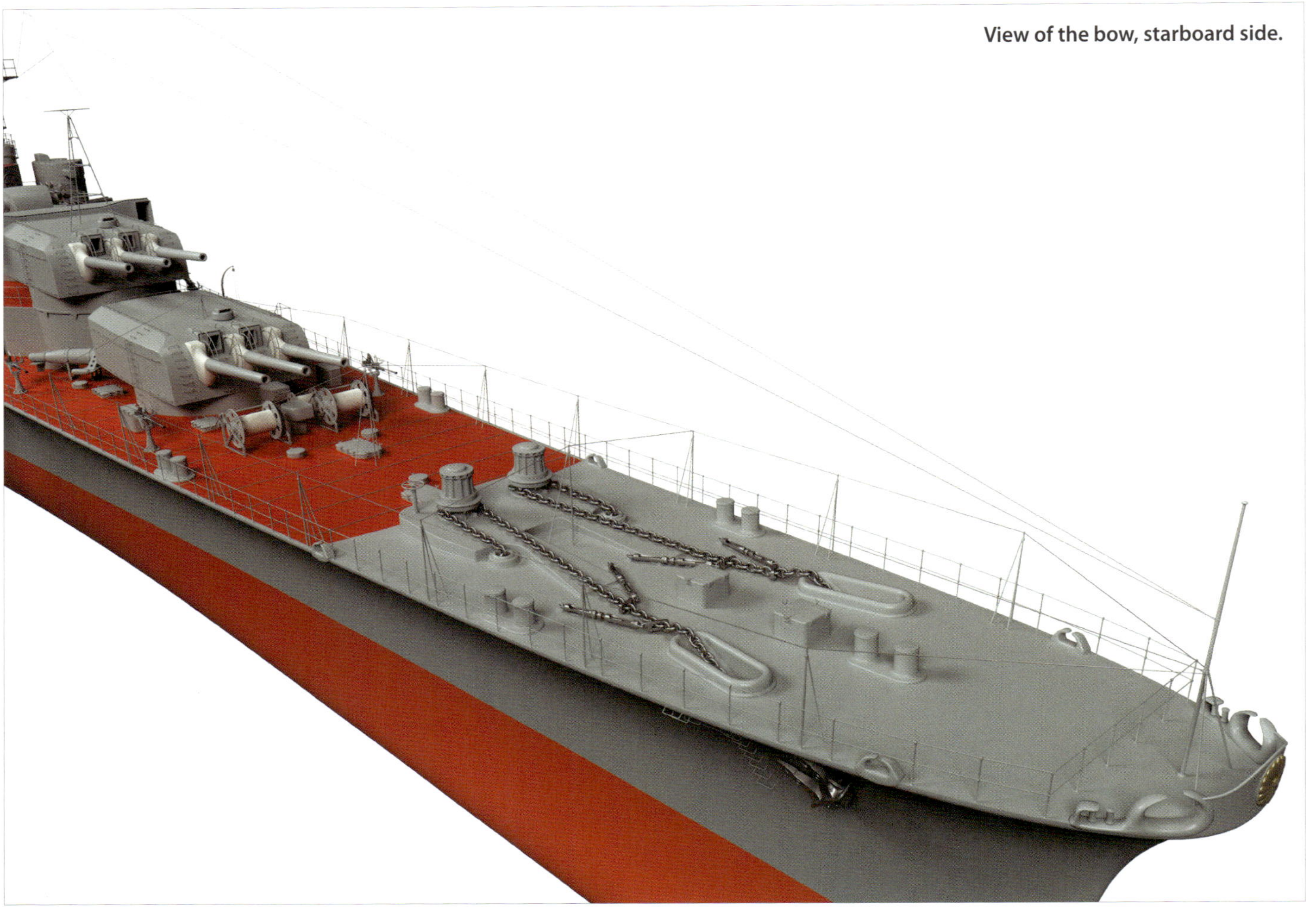

View of the bow, starboard side.

View of the turrets of 155mm guns, starboard side.

View of the turrets of 155mm guns, starboard side.

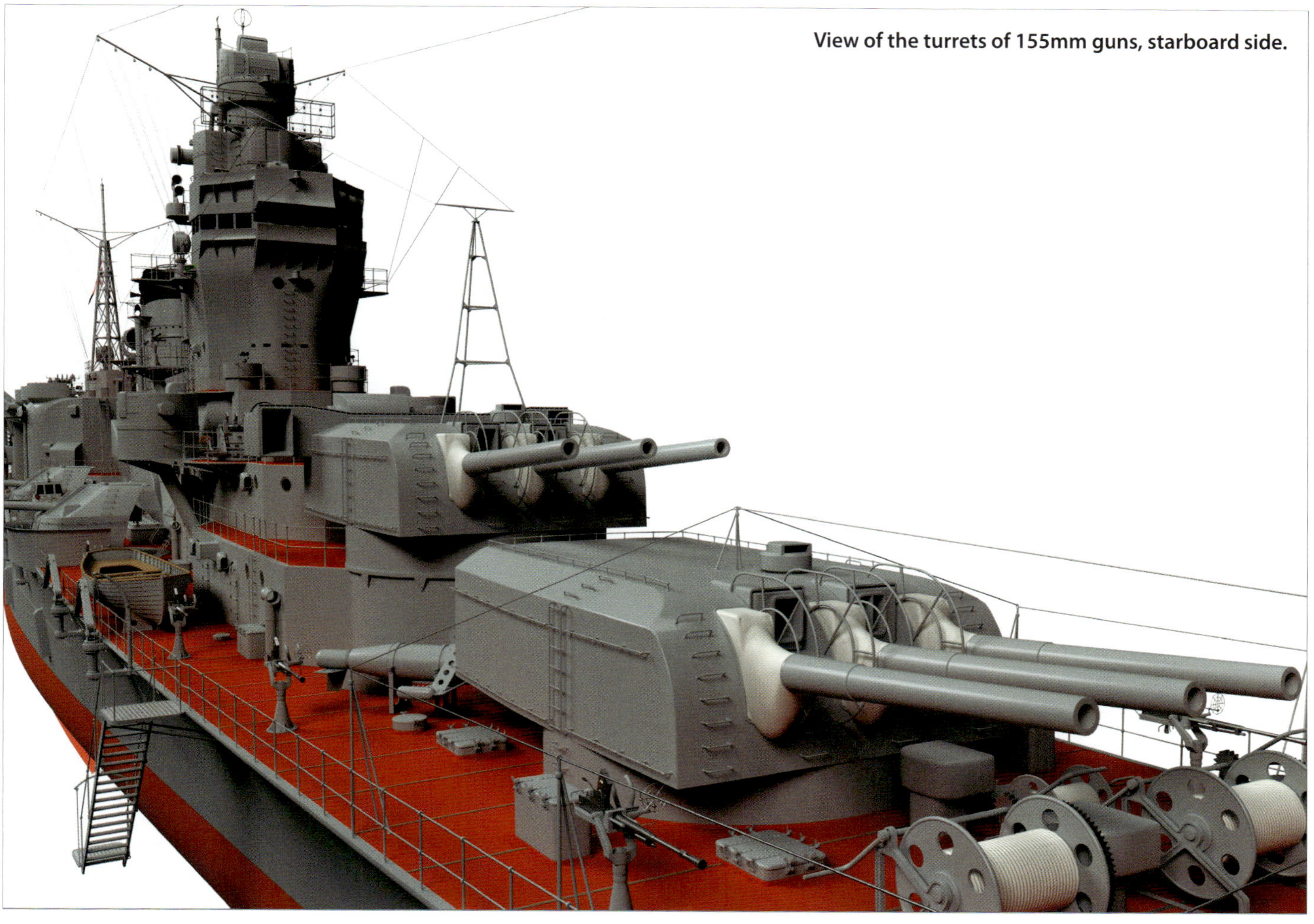
View of the turrets of 155mm guns, starboard side.

View of the center part of the ship, starboard side.

View of the forward superstructure of the ship, starboard side.

View of the ship's chimney, starboard side.

View of the aircraft hangar, starboard side.

View of the aft part of the ship, starboard side.

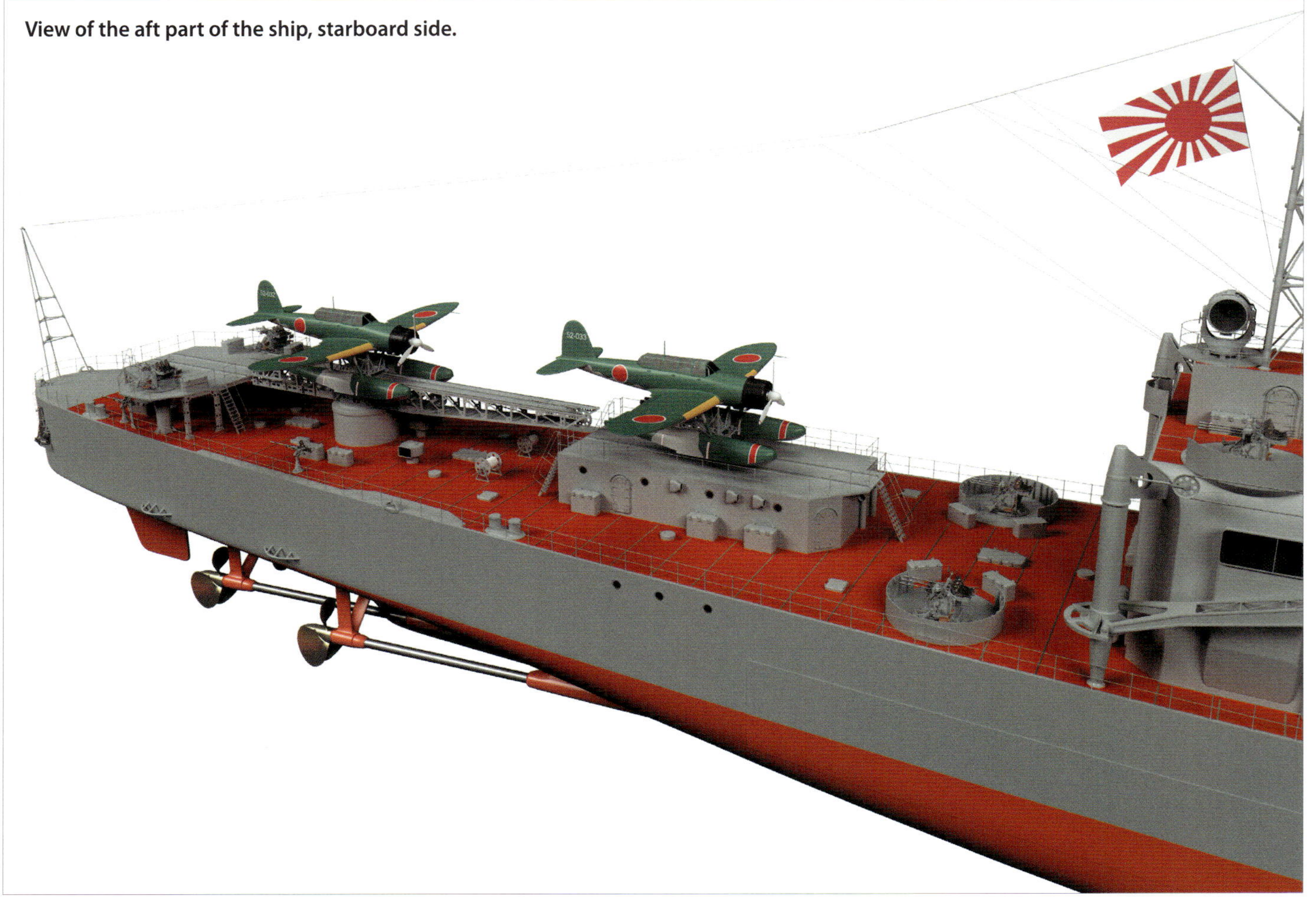

View of the bow of the ship, starboard side.

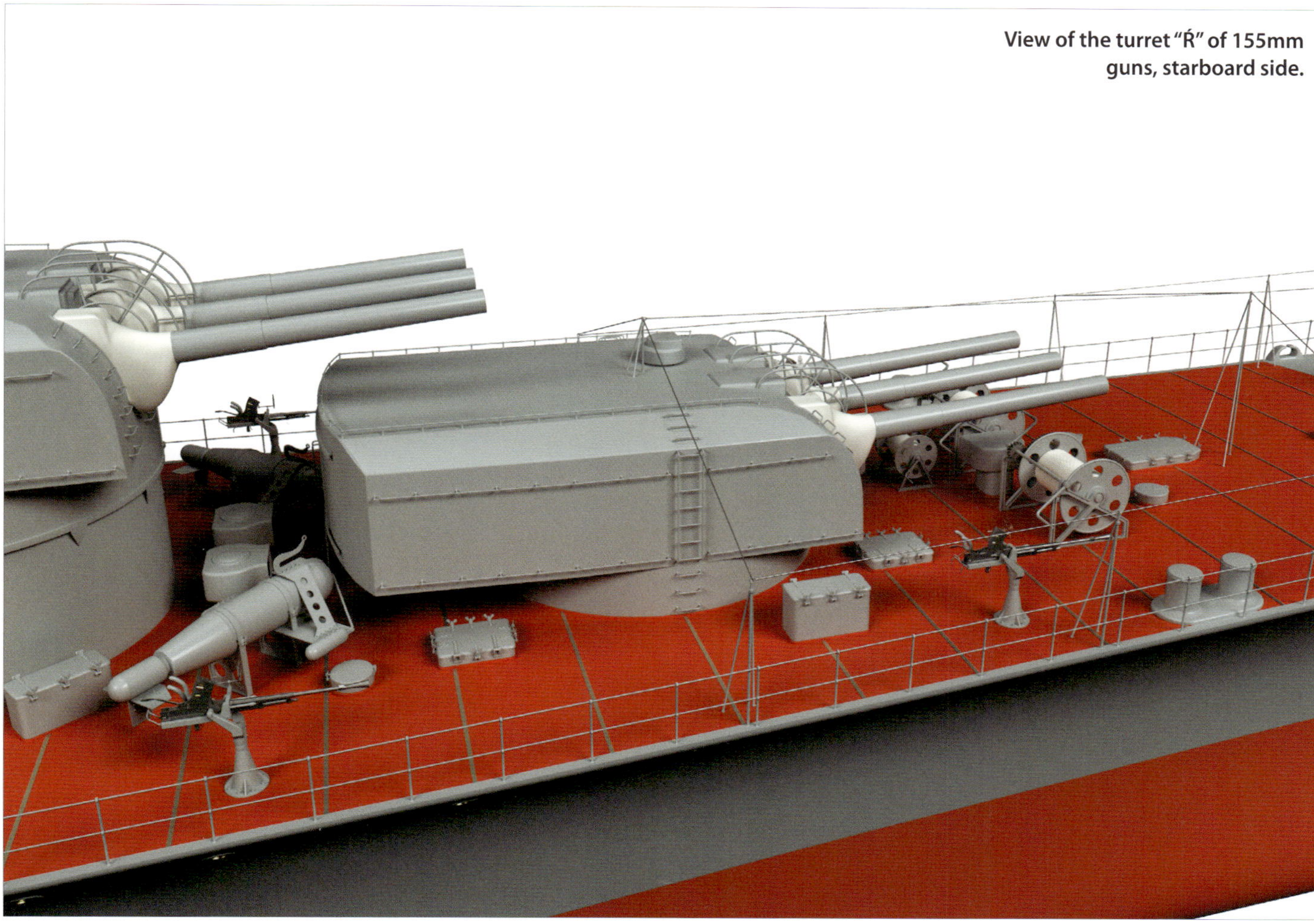

View of the turret "Ŕ" of 155mm guns, starboard side.

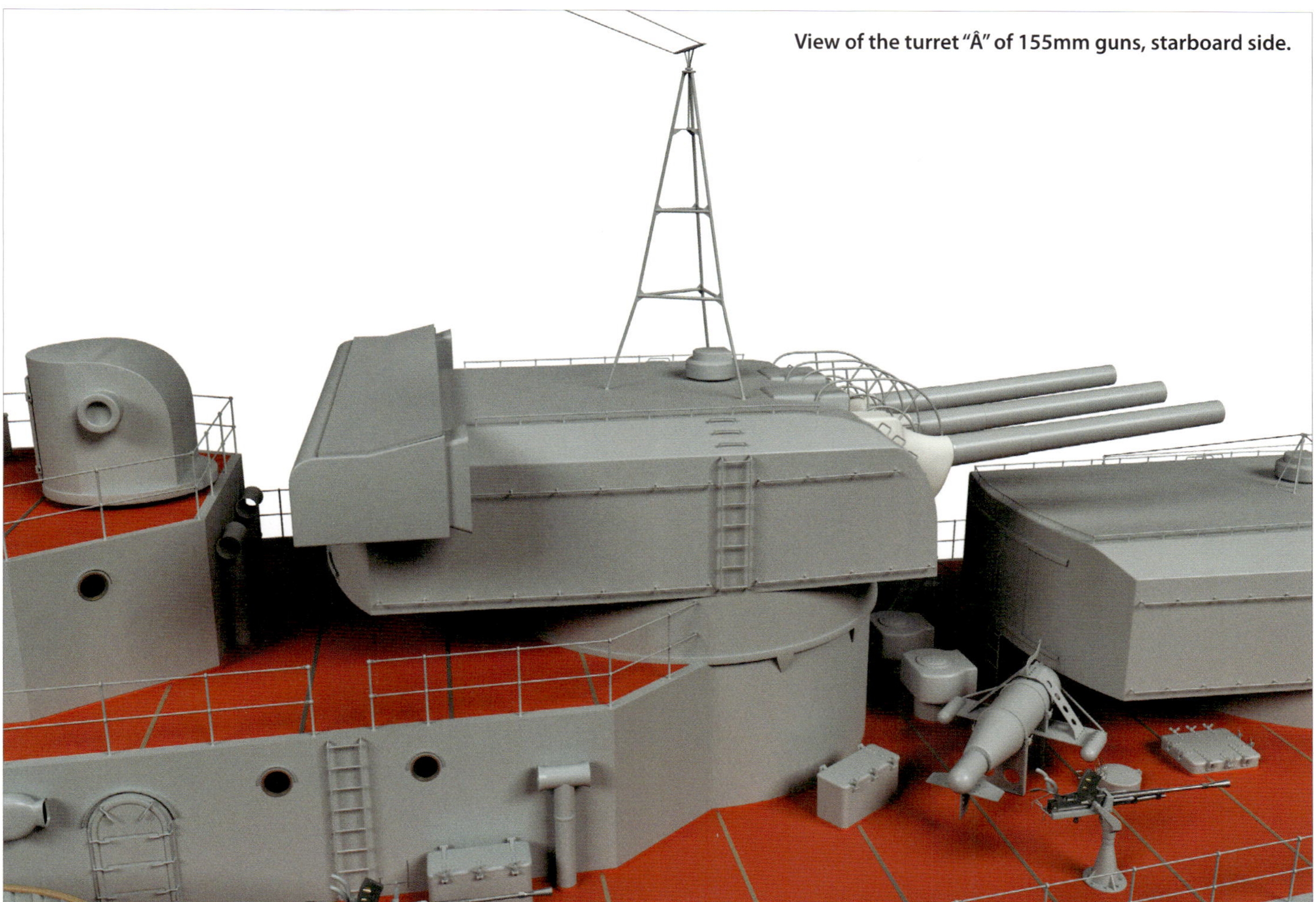

View of the turret "Â" of 155mm guns, starboard side.

View of the turrets of 155mm guns, starboard side.

View of the turret "B" of 155mm guns, starboard side.

View of the turret "B" of 155mm guns, starboard side.

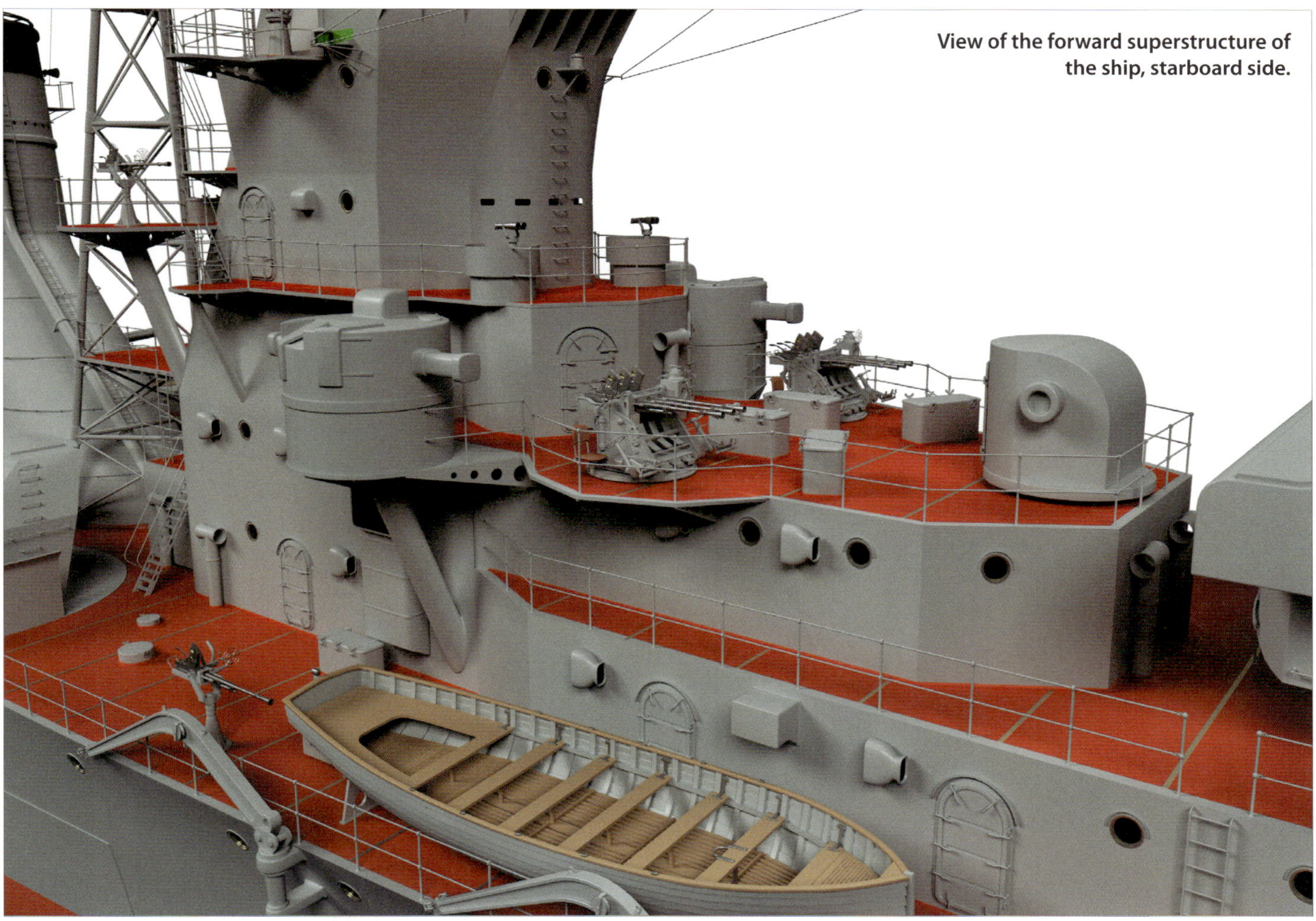

View of the forward superstructure of the ship, starboard side.

View of the forward superstructure of the ship, starboard side.

View of the ship's radar station, starboard side.

View of the observation post, starboard side.

View of the forward superstructure of the ship, starboard side.

View of the rangefinder, starboard side.

View of the forward superstructure of the ship, starboard side.

View of the forward superstructure of the ship, starboard side.

View of the lifeboat, starboard side.

View of the turret "B" of 155mm guns, starboard side.

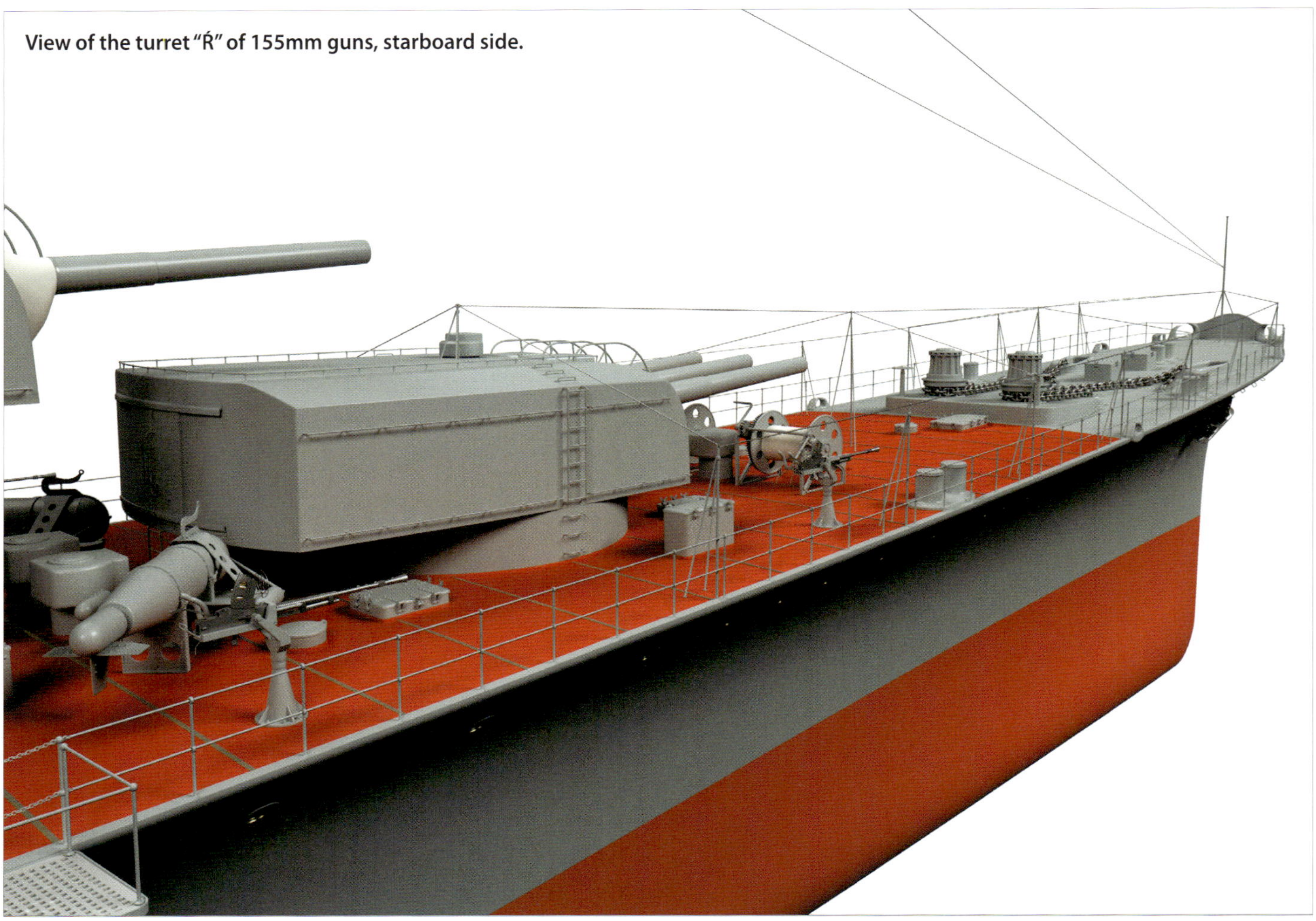

View of the turret "Ŕ" of 155mm guns, starboard side.

View of the universal installation of 100 mm guns, starboard side.

View of the universal installation of 100 mm guns, starboard side.

▲
View of the motor boat, starboard side.

View of the chimney, starboard side.
▼

View of the chimney, starboard side.

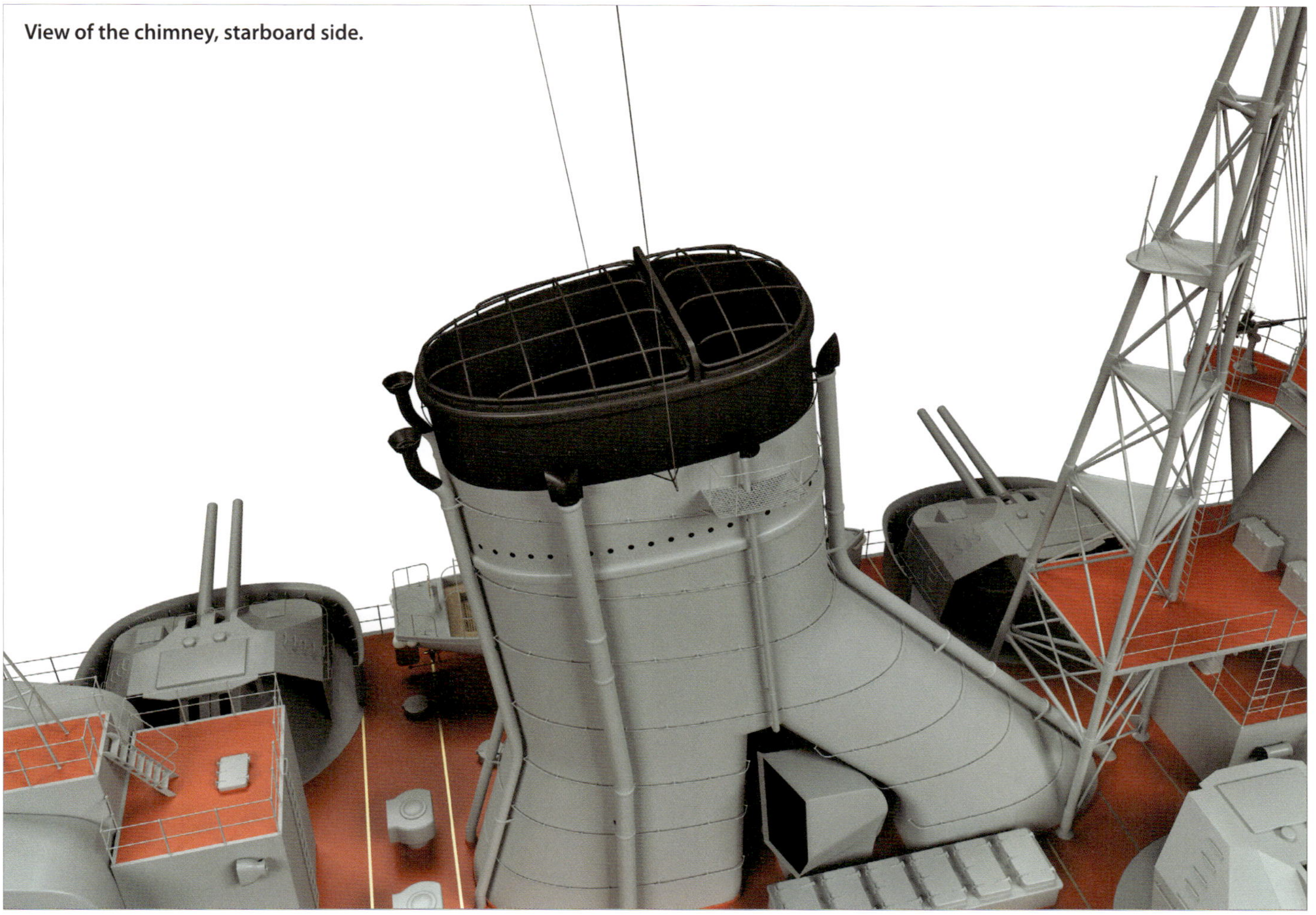

View of the chimney, starboard side.

Overall view of the central part of the ship, starboard side.

View of the motor boat, starboard side.

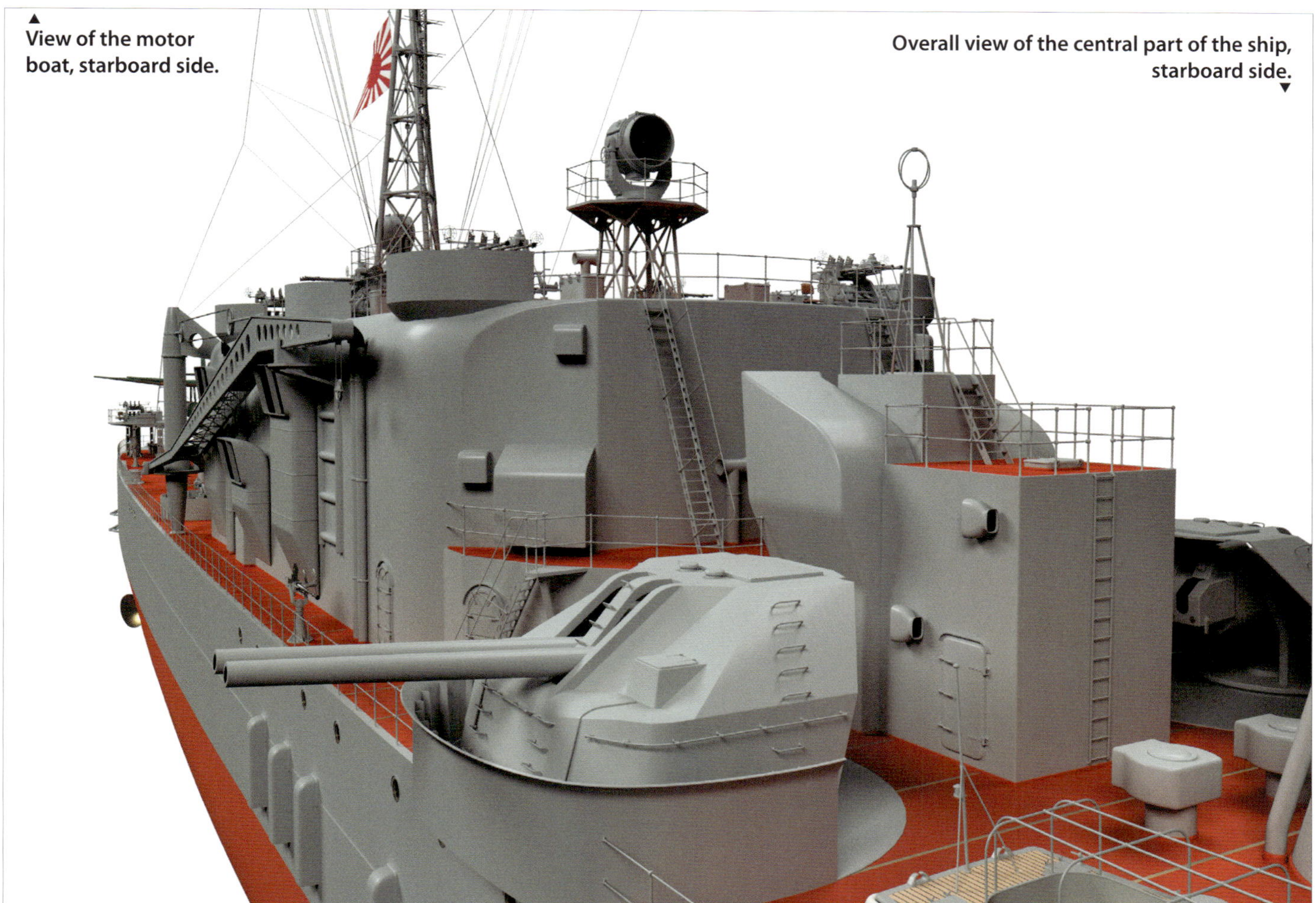

▲ View of the motor boat, starboard side.

Overall view of the central part of the ship, starboard side. ▼

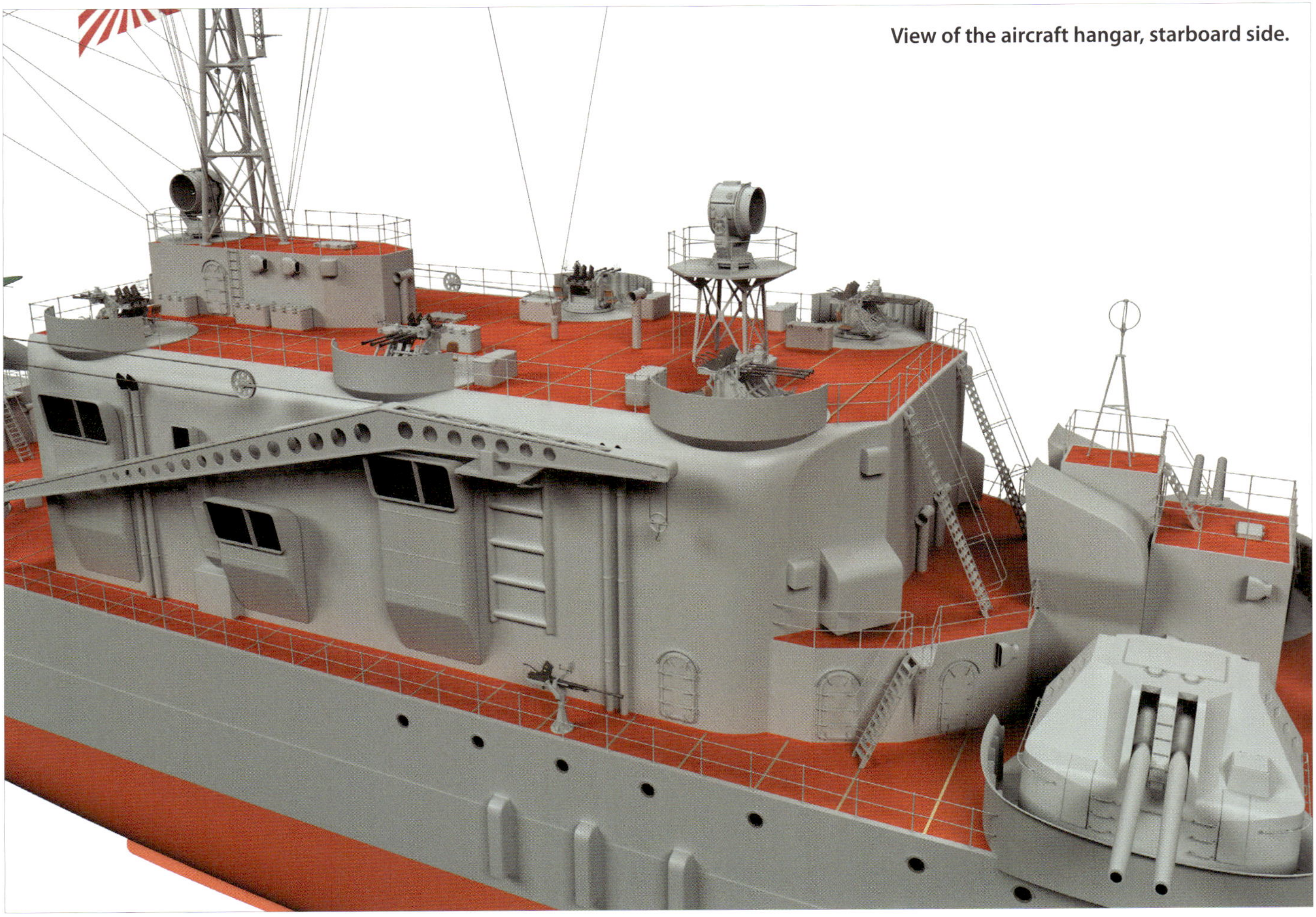

View of the aircraft hangar, starboard side.

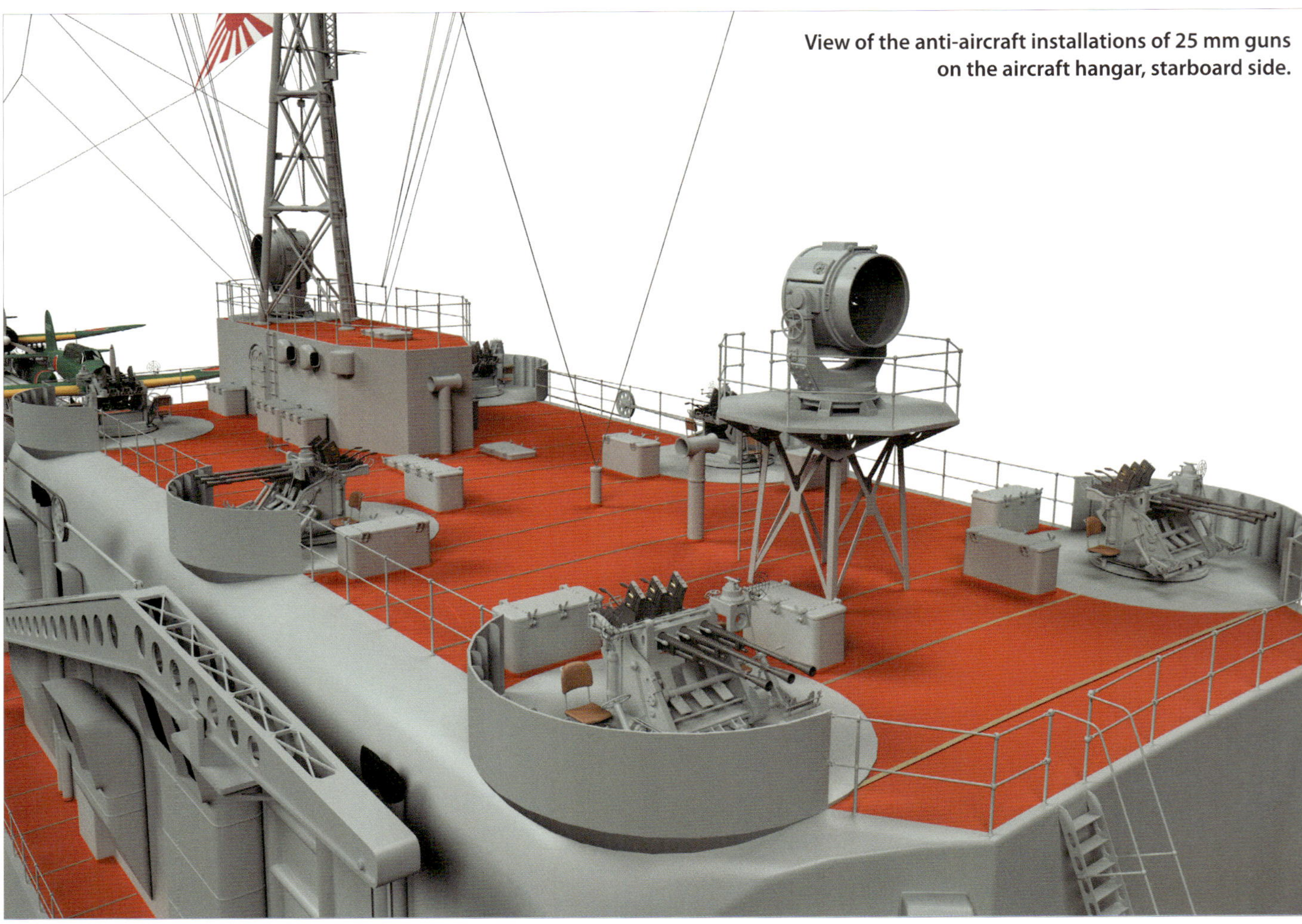

View of the anti-aircraft installations of 25 mm guns on the aircraft hangar, starboard side.

View of the radio room and searchlight, starboard side.

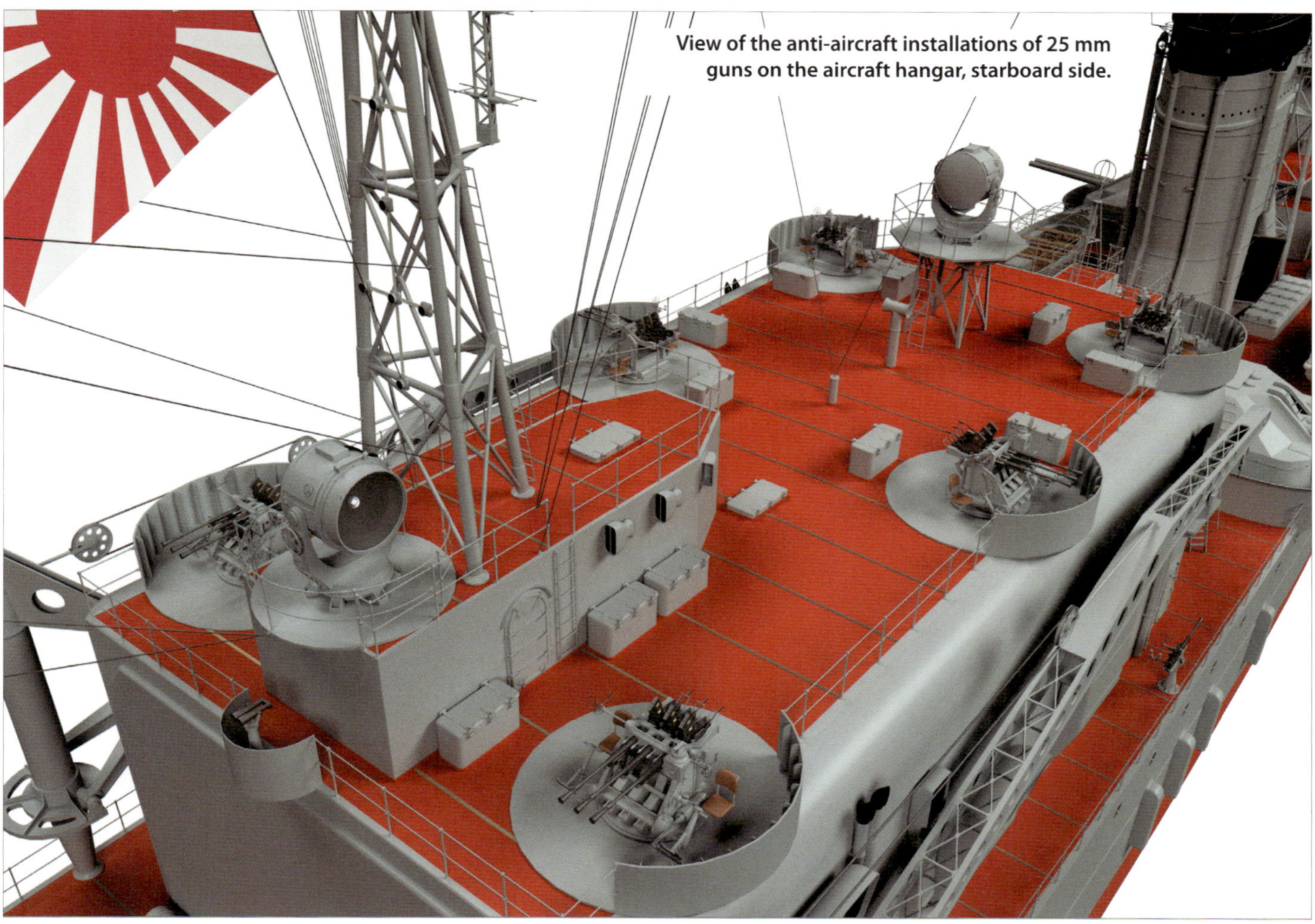
View of the anti-aircraft installations of 25 mm guns on the aircraft hangar, starboard side.

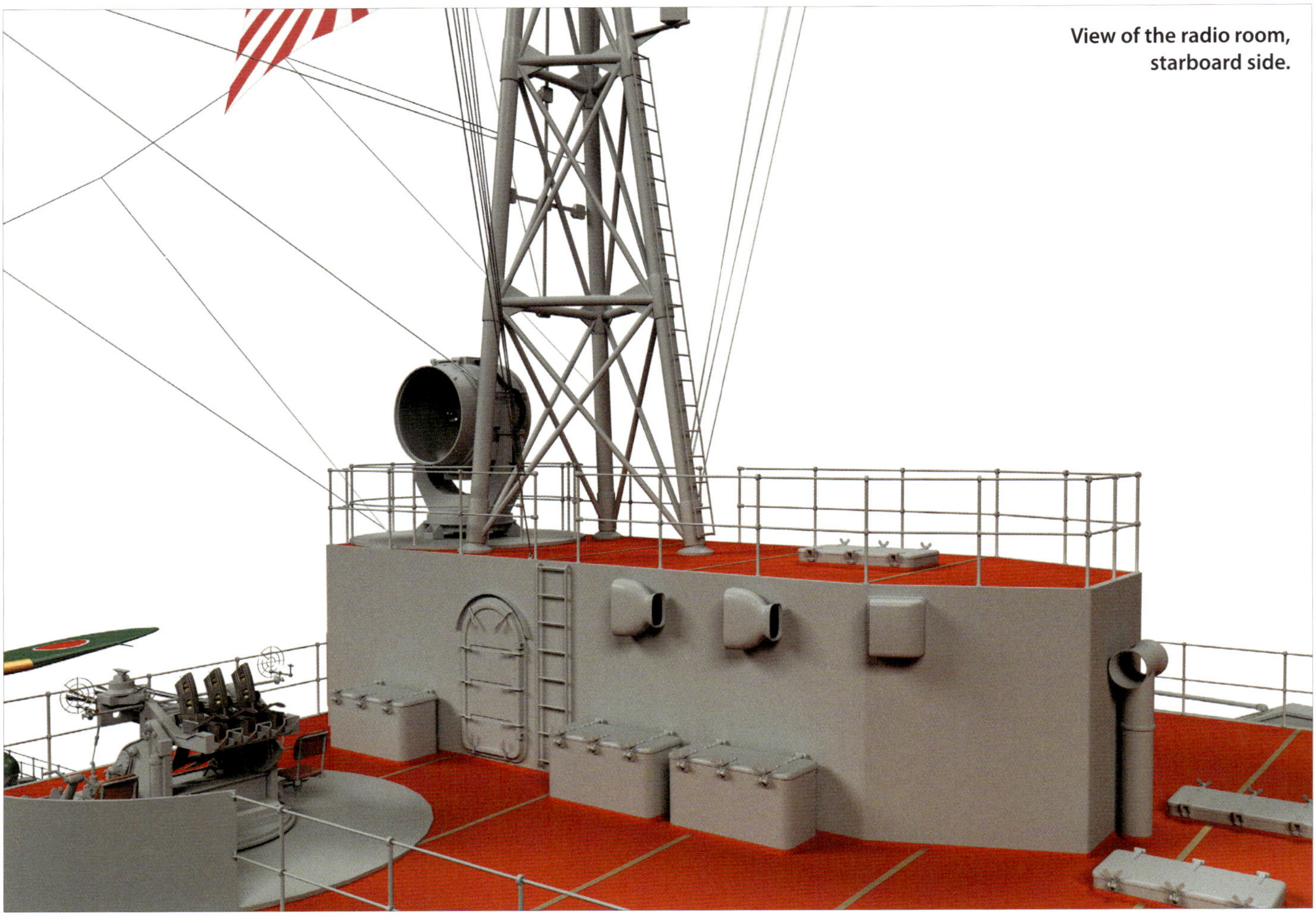

View of the radio room, starboard side.

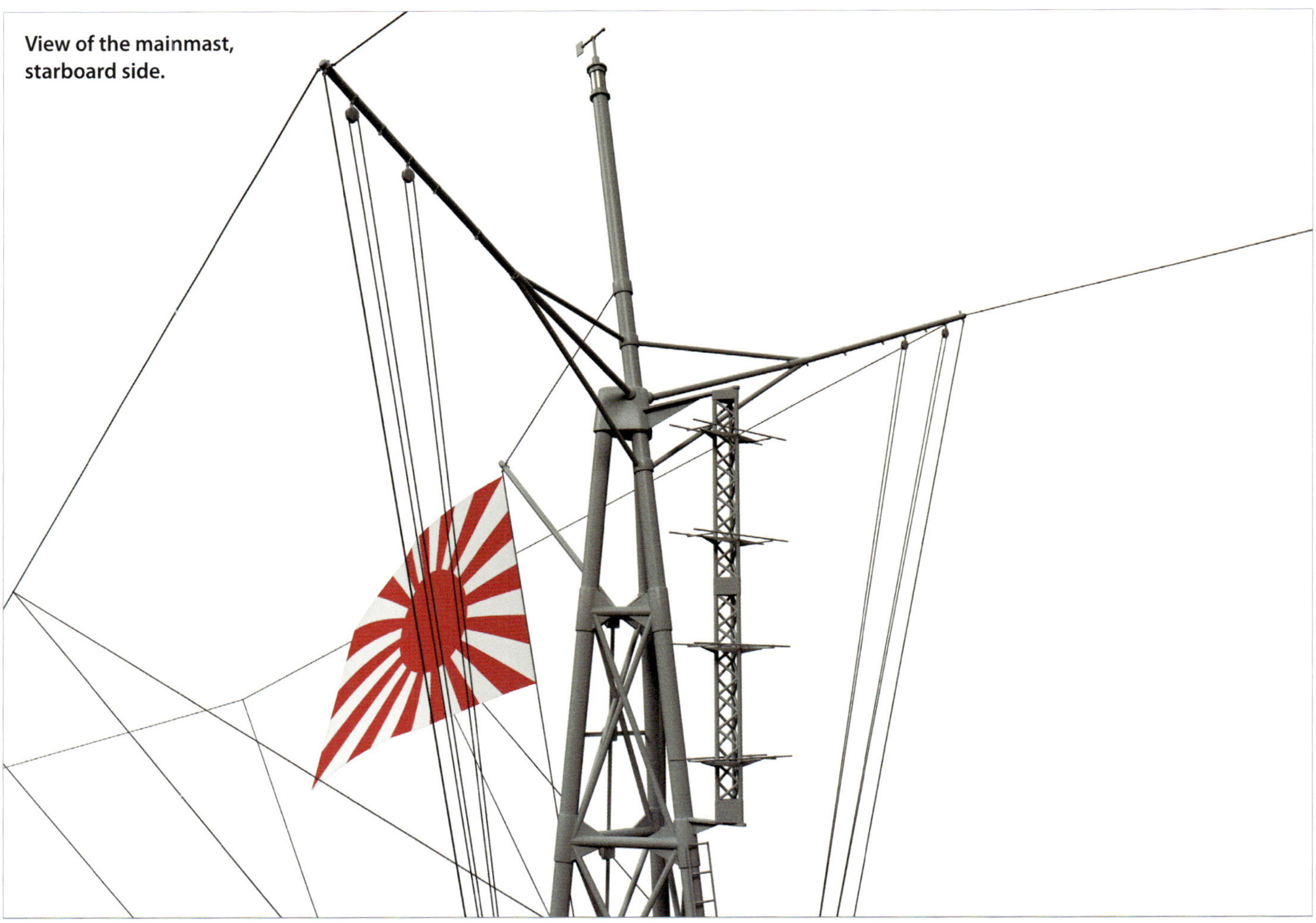

View of the mainmast, starboard side.

View of the aircraft hangar, starboard side.

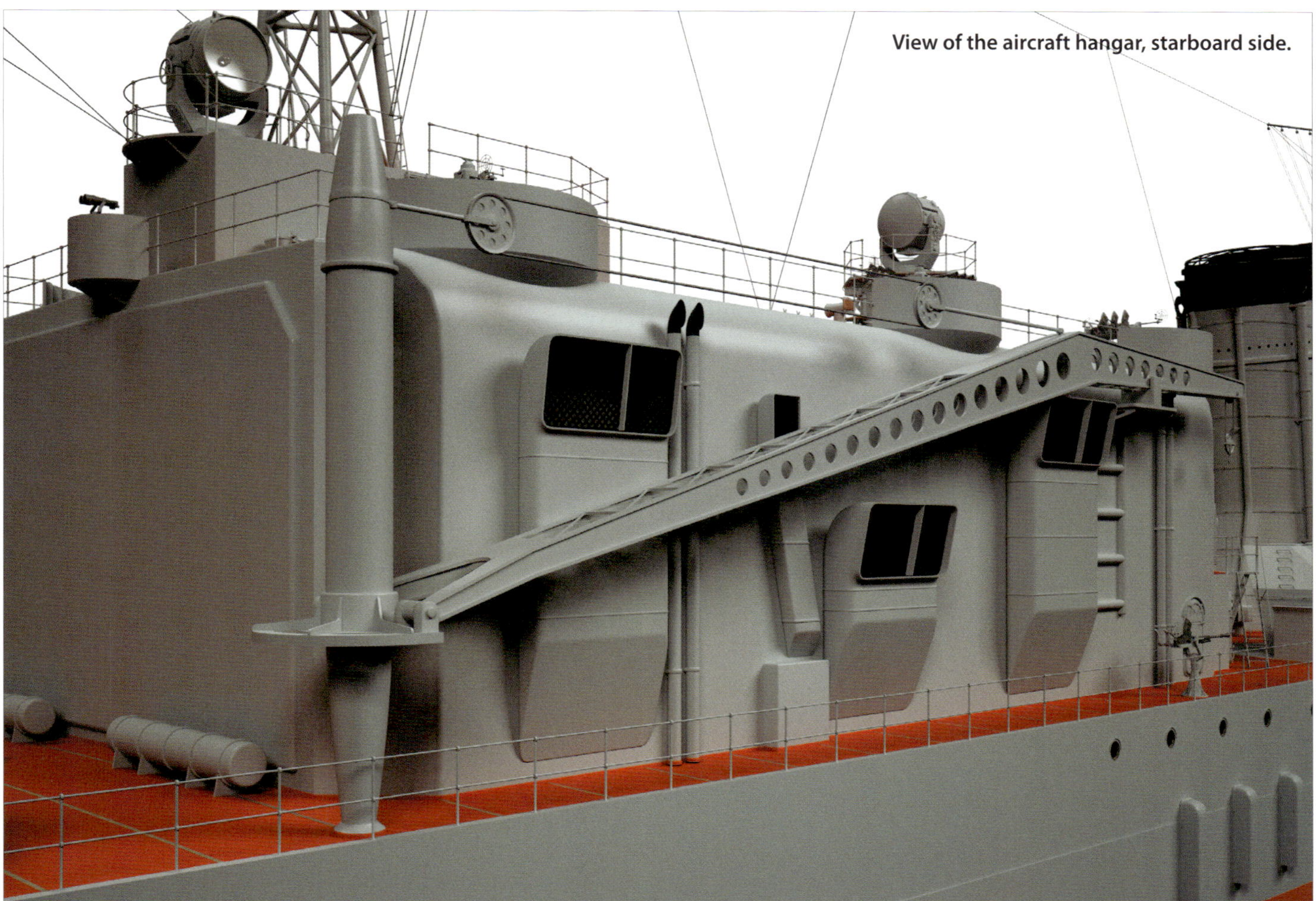

View of the aircraft hangar, starboard side.

View of the reconnaissance aircraft No. 1, starboard side.

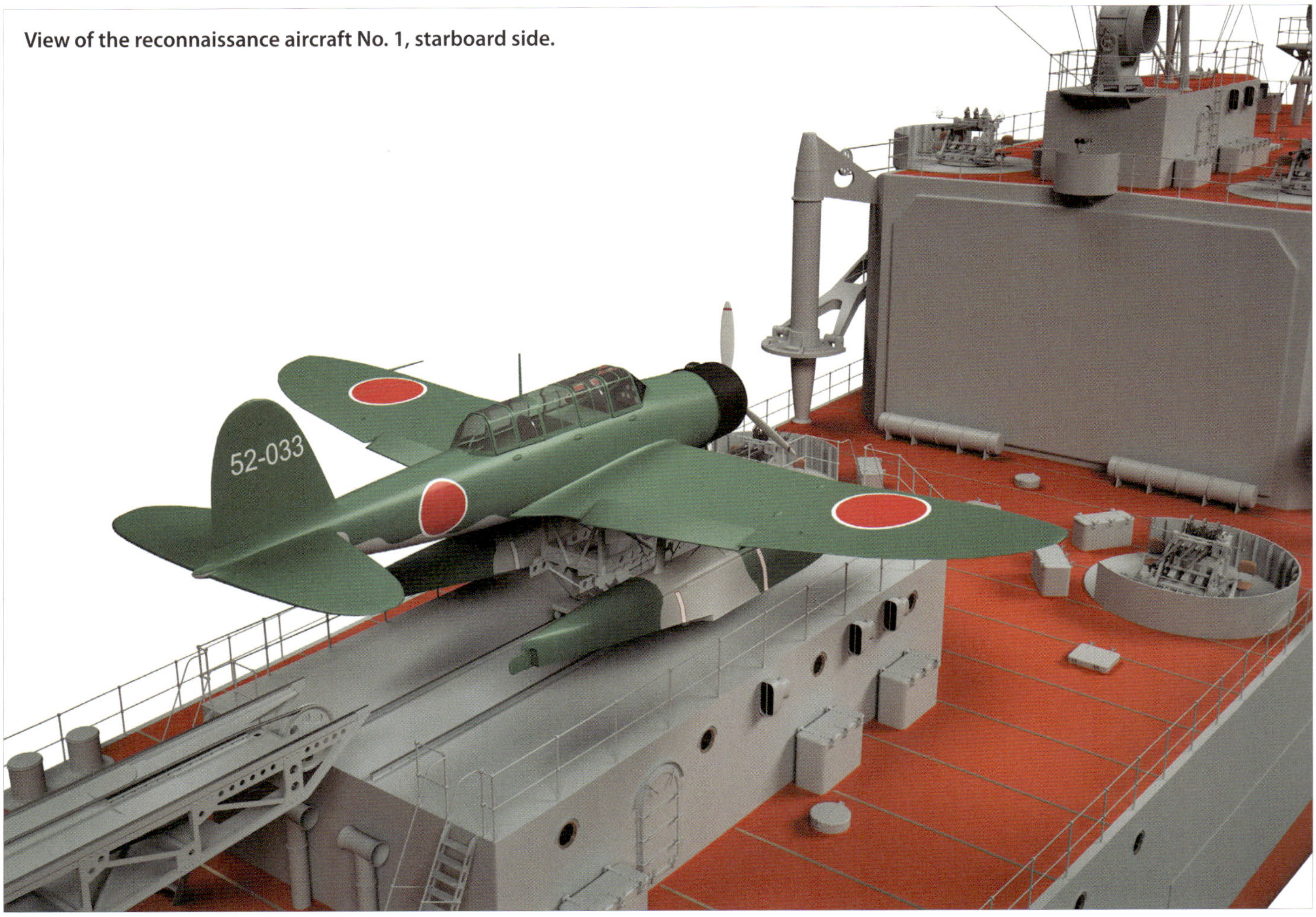

View of the reconnaissance aircraft No. 2, starboard side.

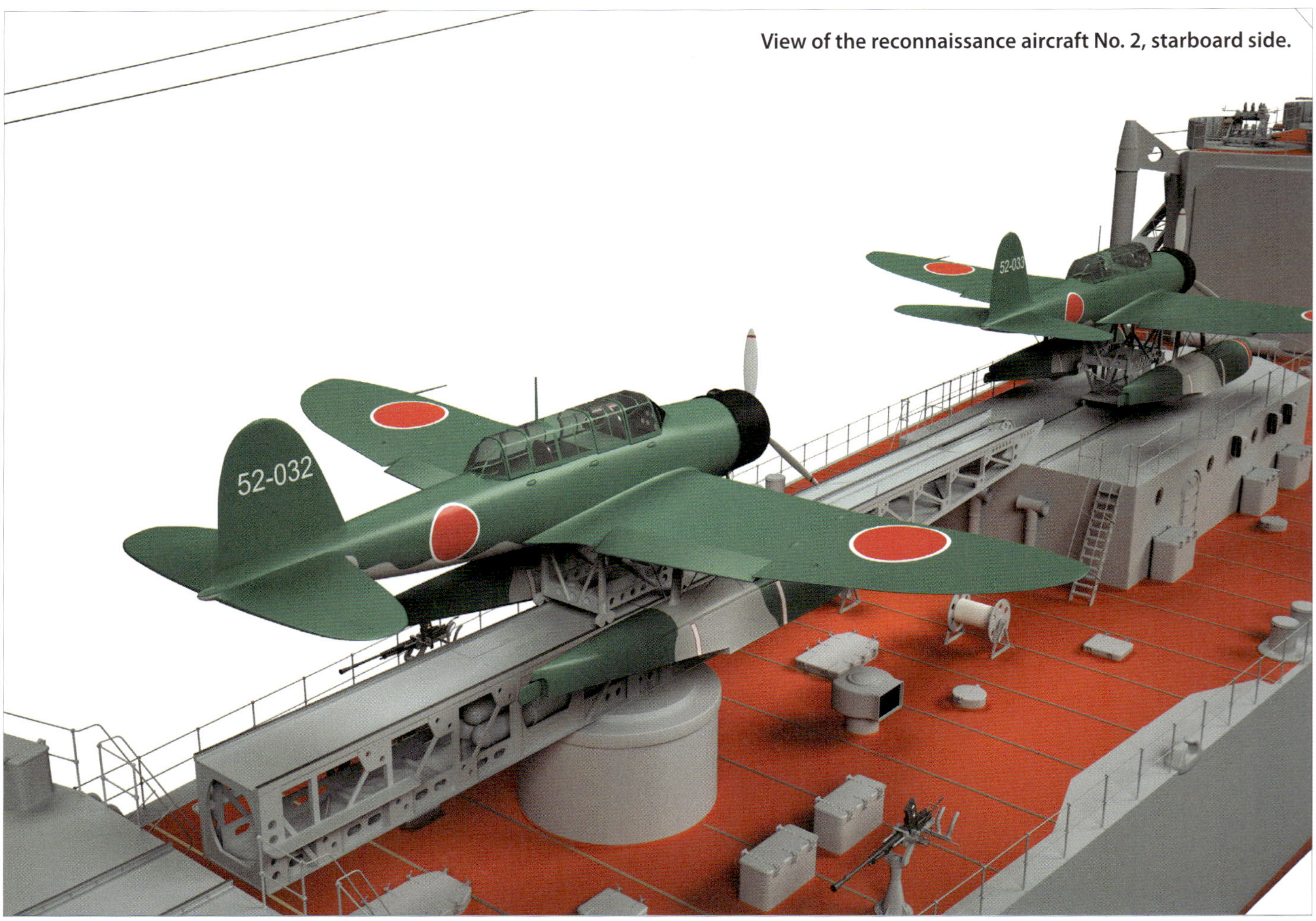

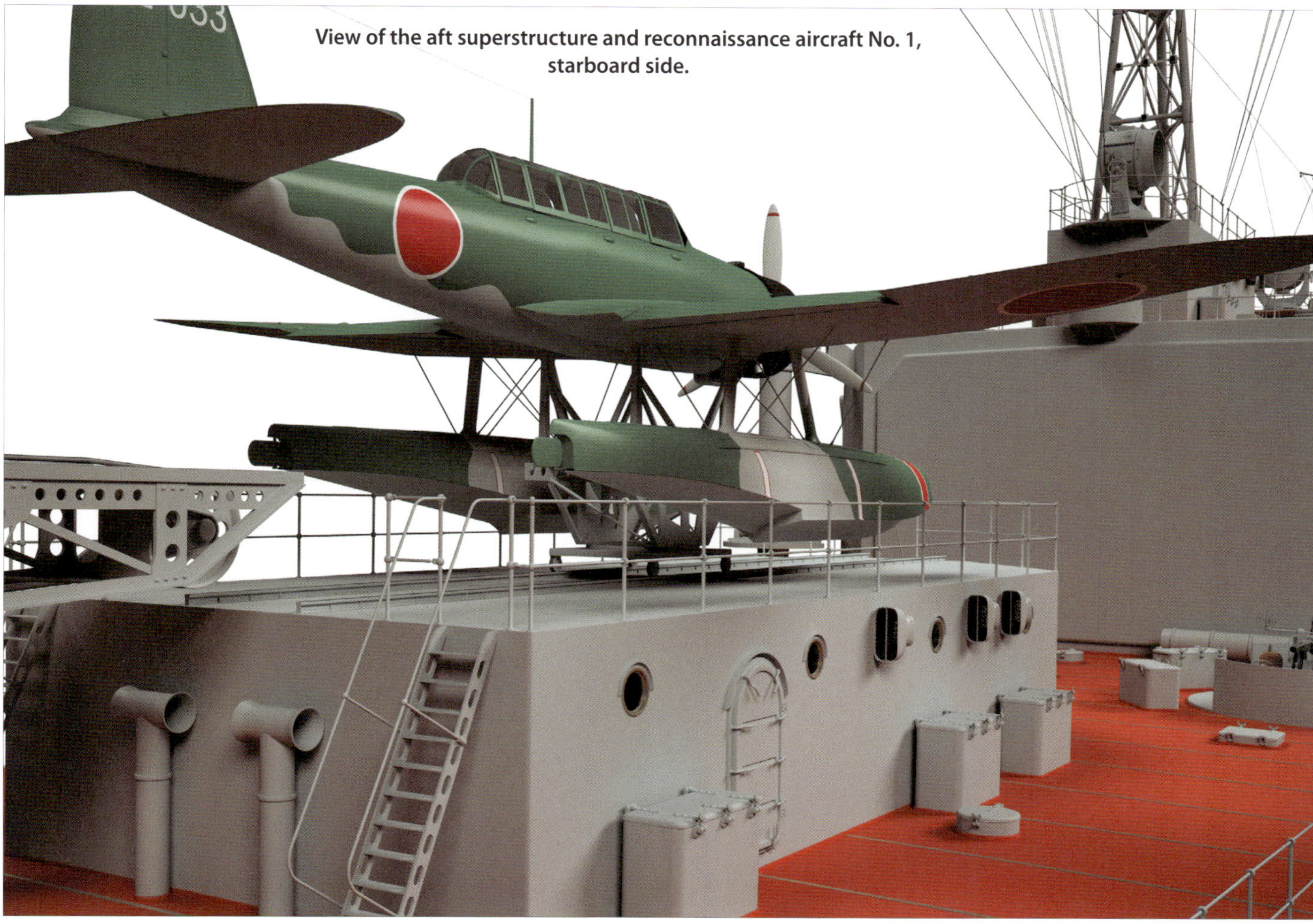

View of the aft superstructure and reconnaissance aircraft No. 1, starboard side.

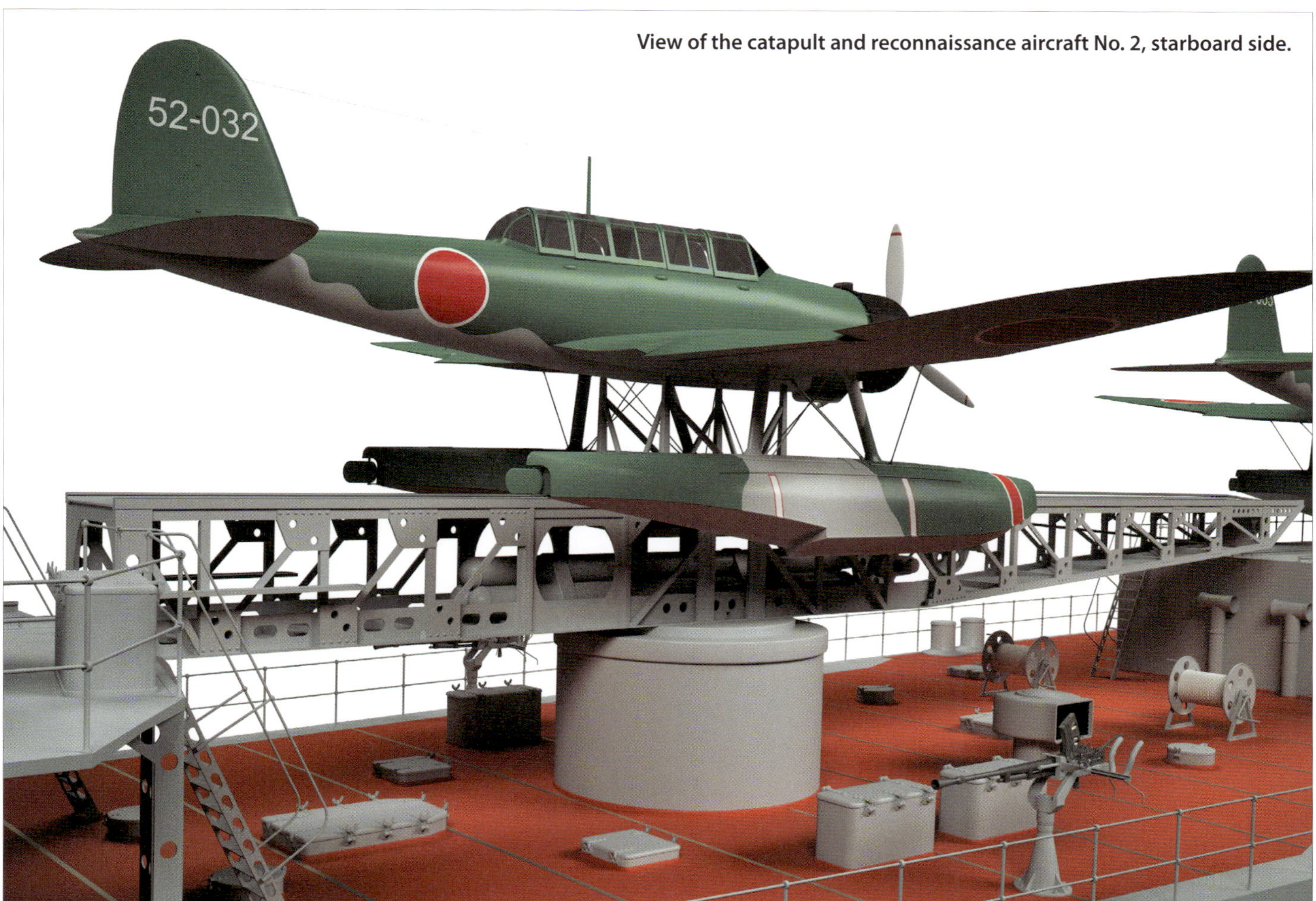

View of the catapult and reconnaissance aircraft No. 2, starboard side.

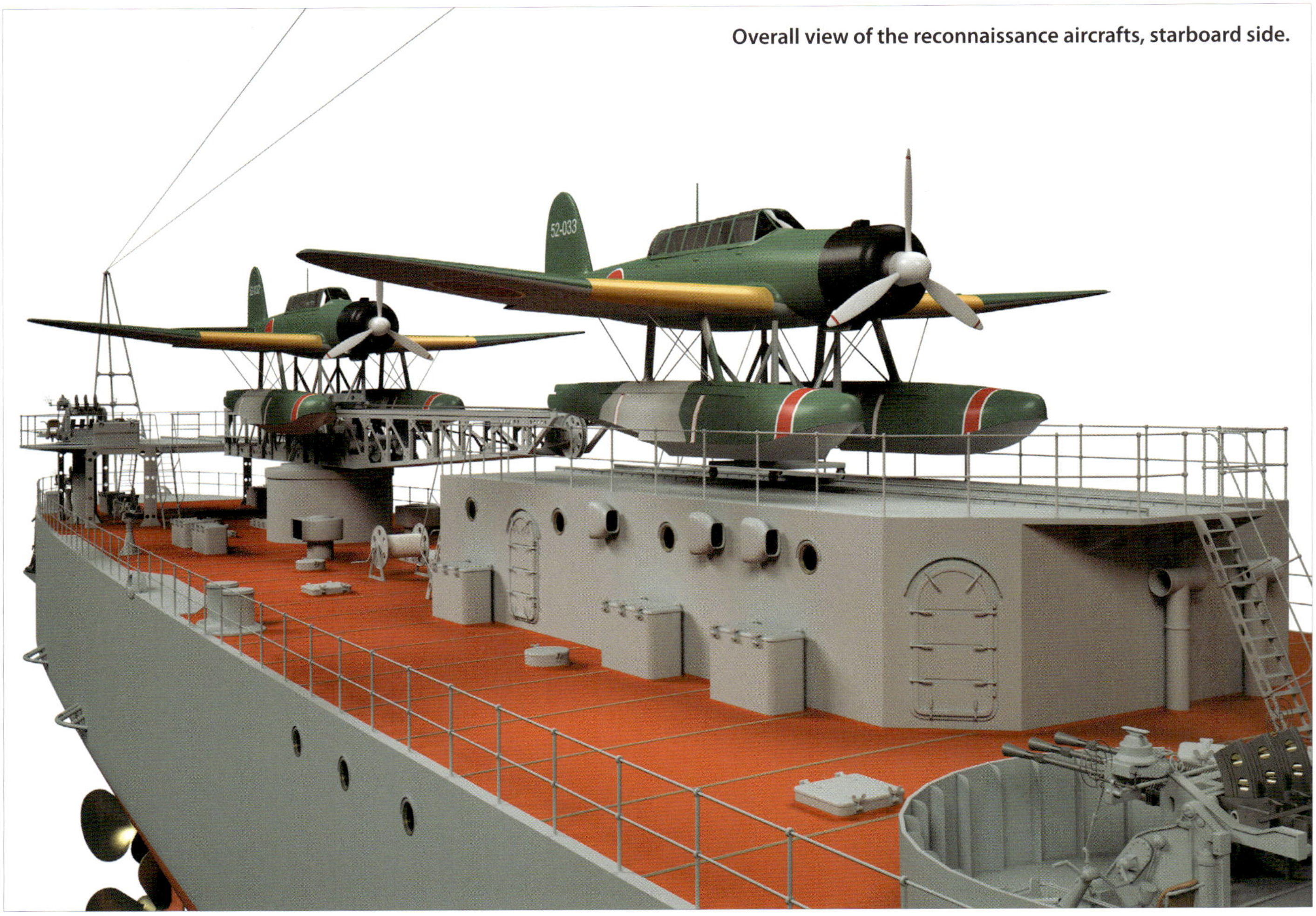

Overall view of the reconnaissance aircrafts, starboard side.

Overall view of the reconnaissance aircrafts, starboard side.

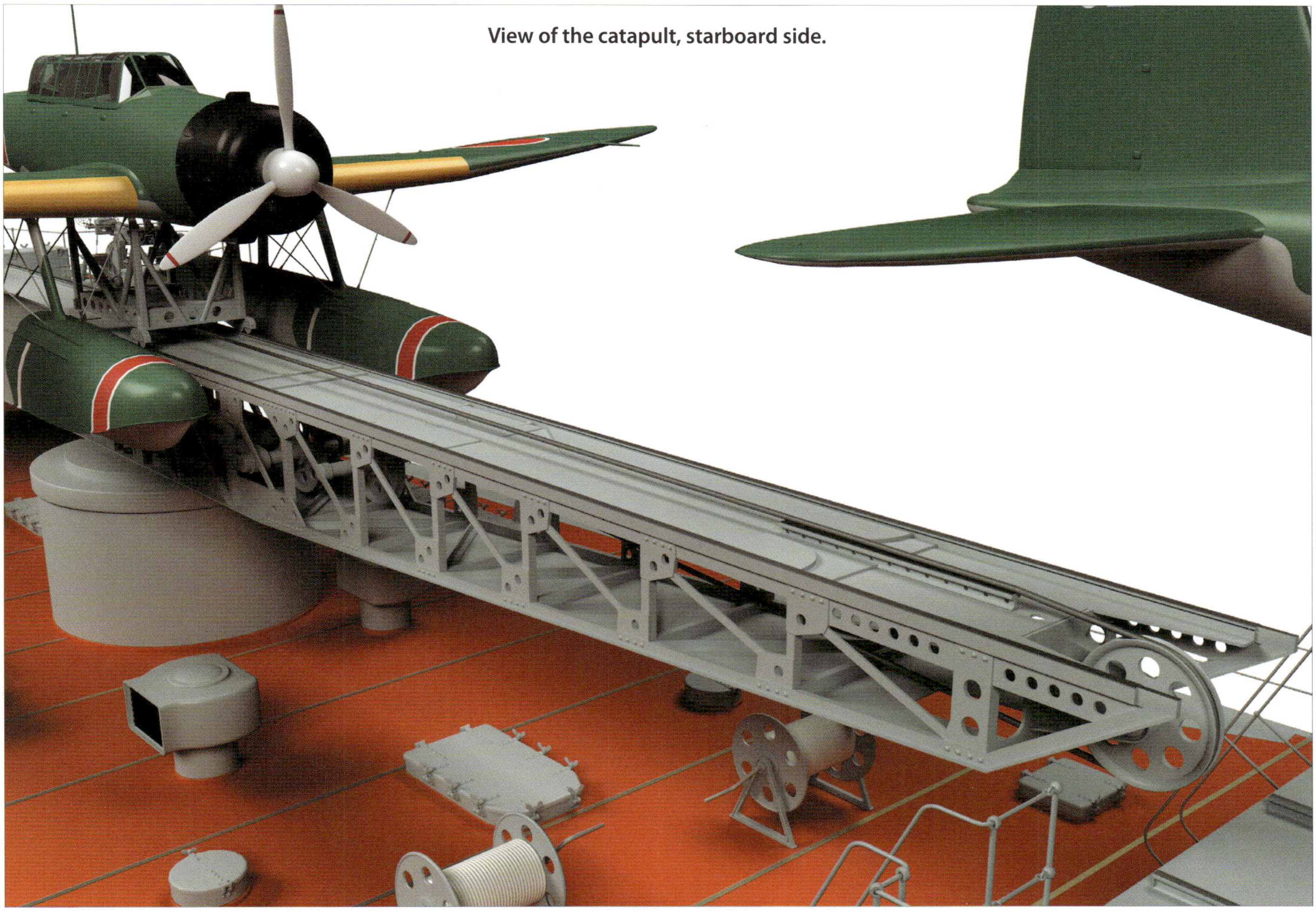

View of the catapult, starboard side.

View of the catapult, starboard side.

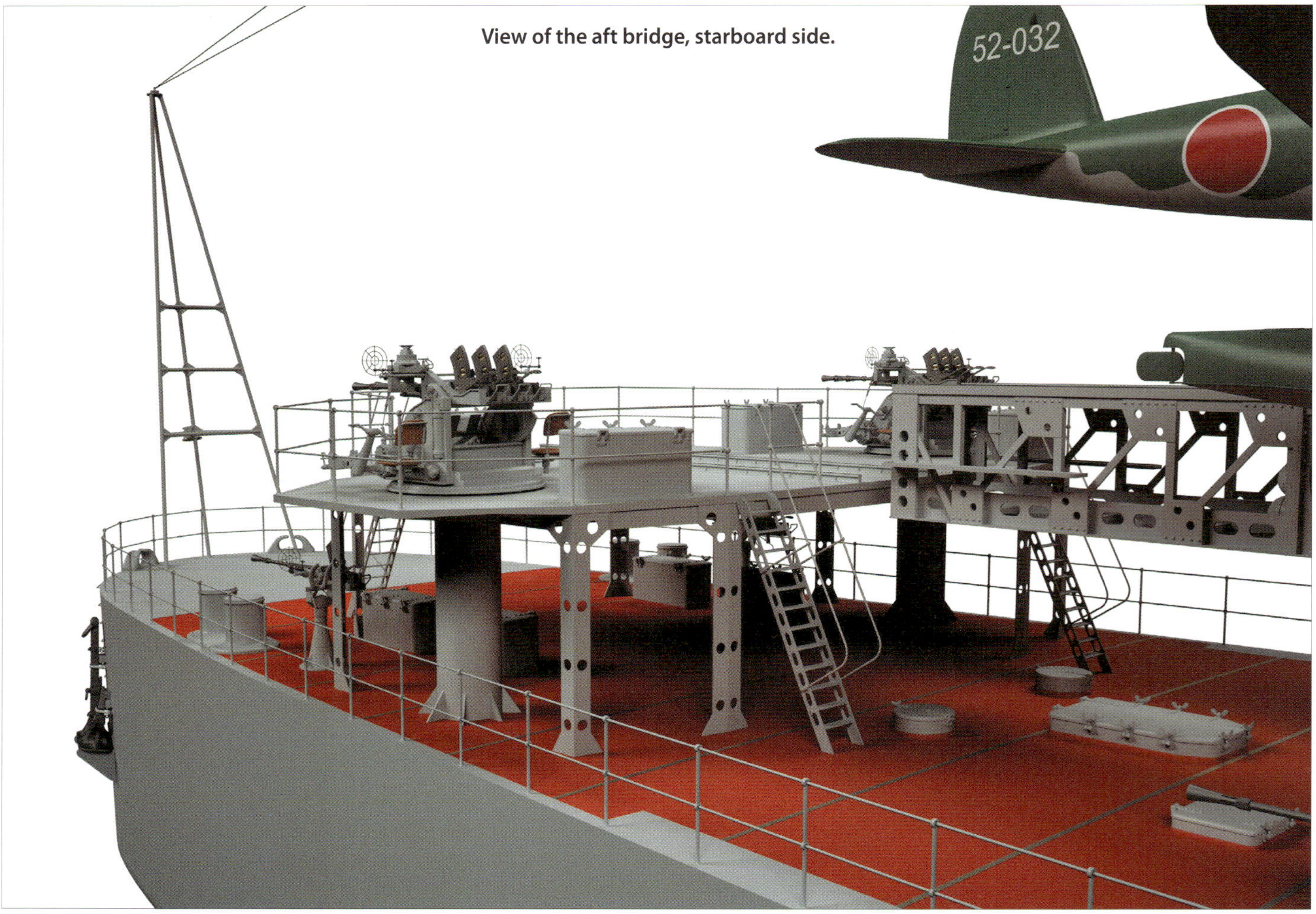

View of the aft bridge, starboard side.

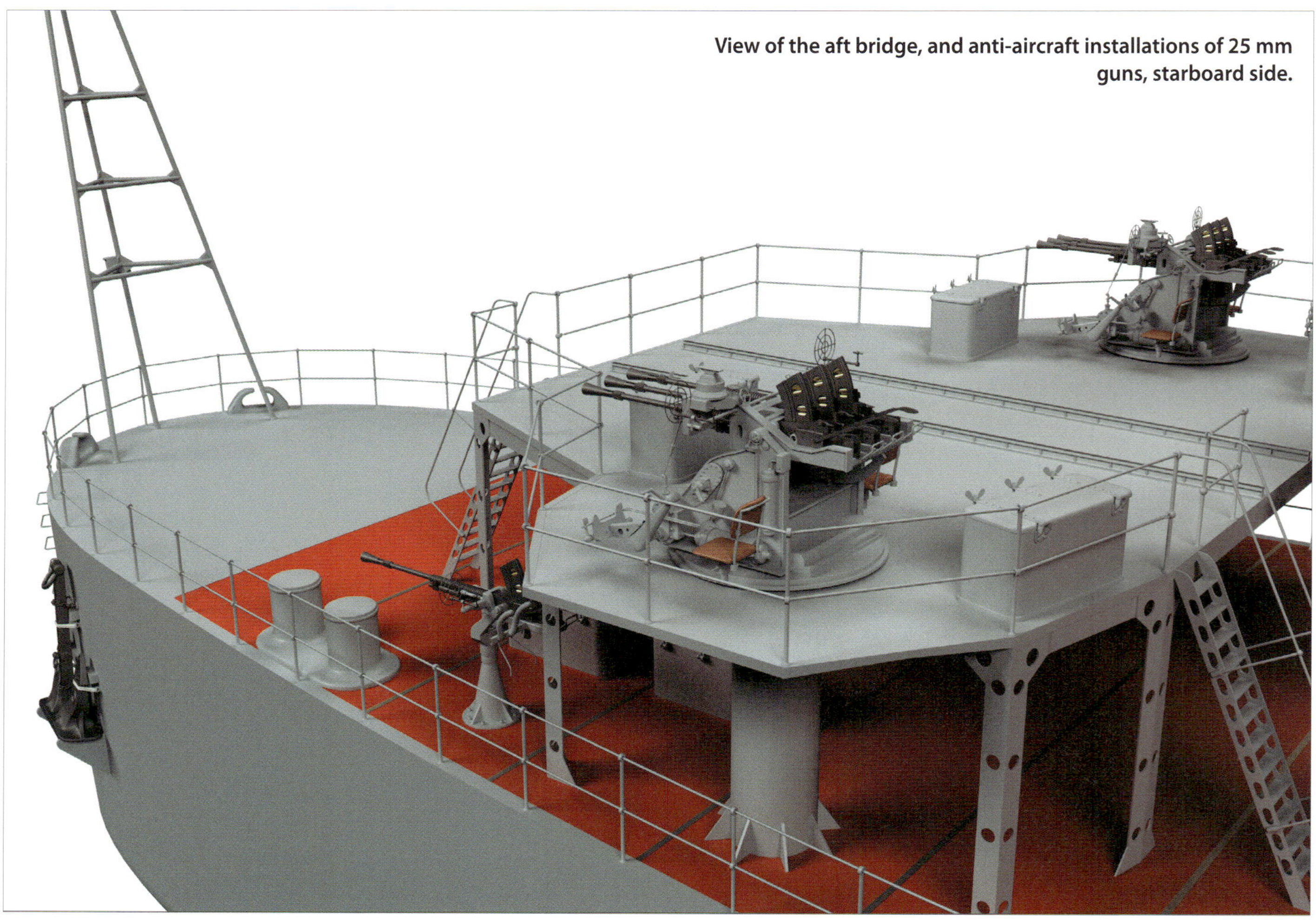
View of the aft bridge, and anti-aircraft installations of 25 mm guns, starboard side.

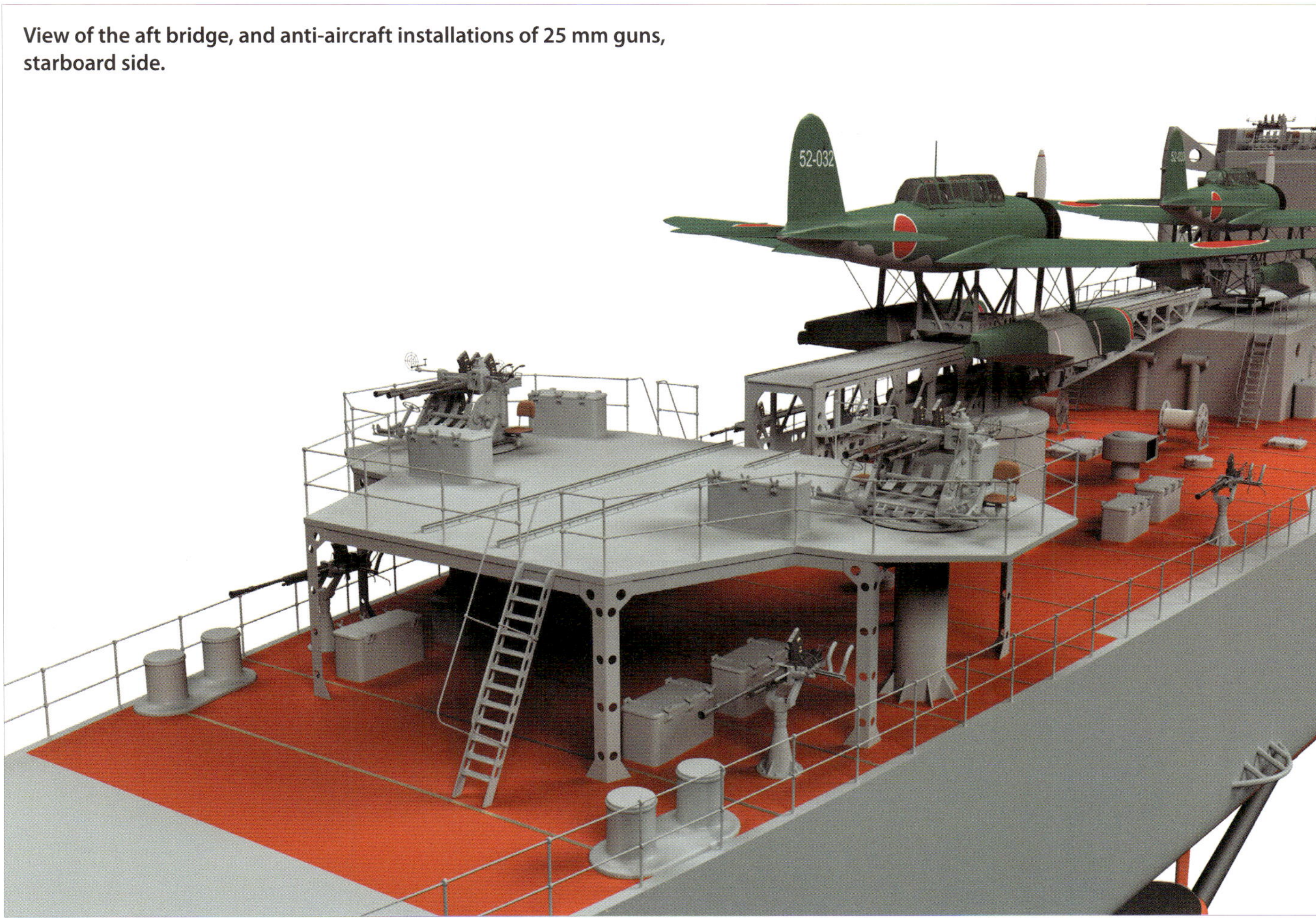

View of the aft bridge, and anti-aircraft installations of 25 mm guns, starboard side.

View of the aft part of the ship, starboard side.

View of the ship's propellers.

Overall view of the ship, starboard side.

Overall view of the ship from the stern, starboard side.

Overall view of the ship, port side.

Overall view of the ship, port side.

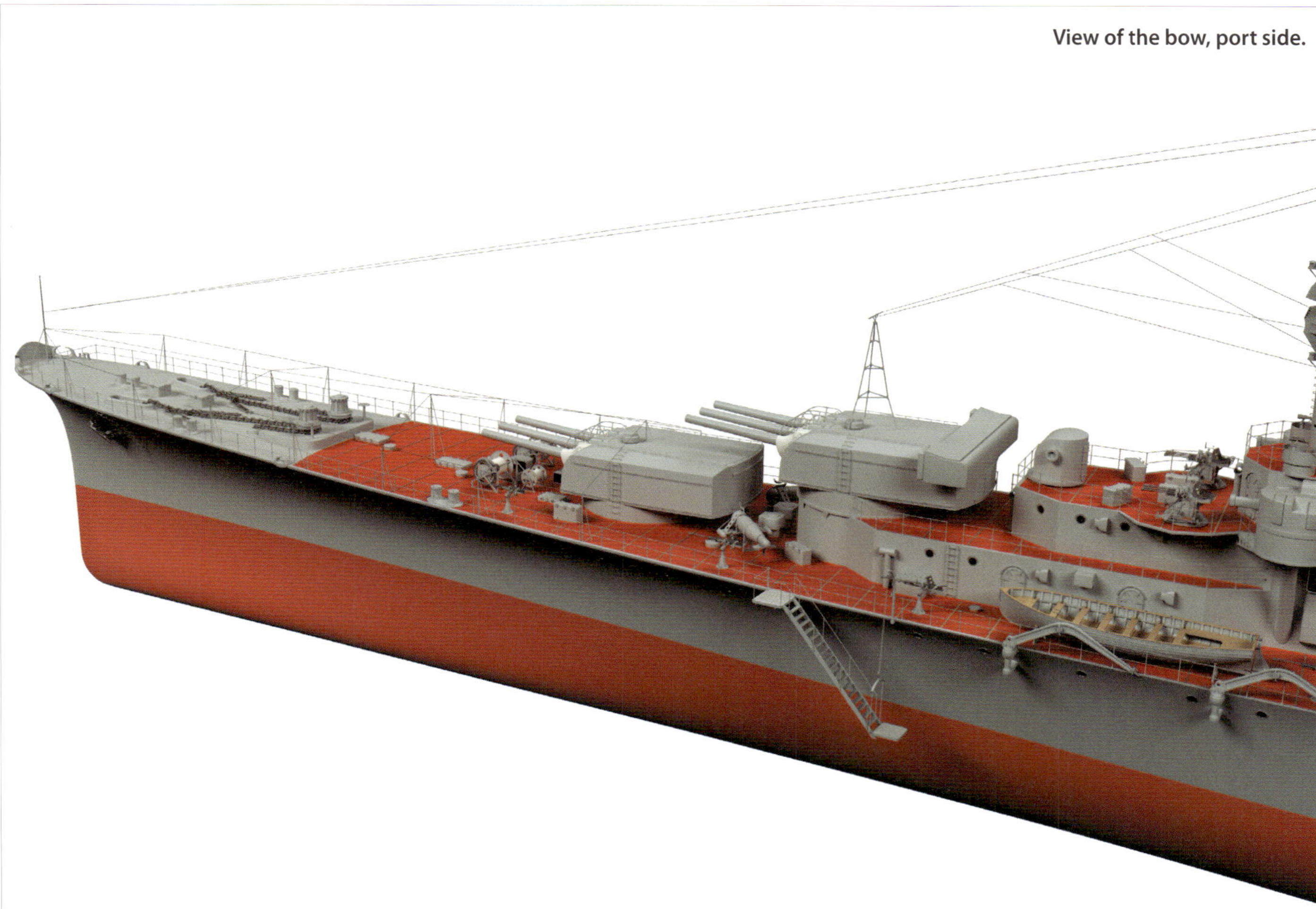

View of the bow, port side.

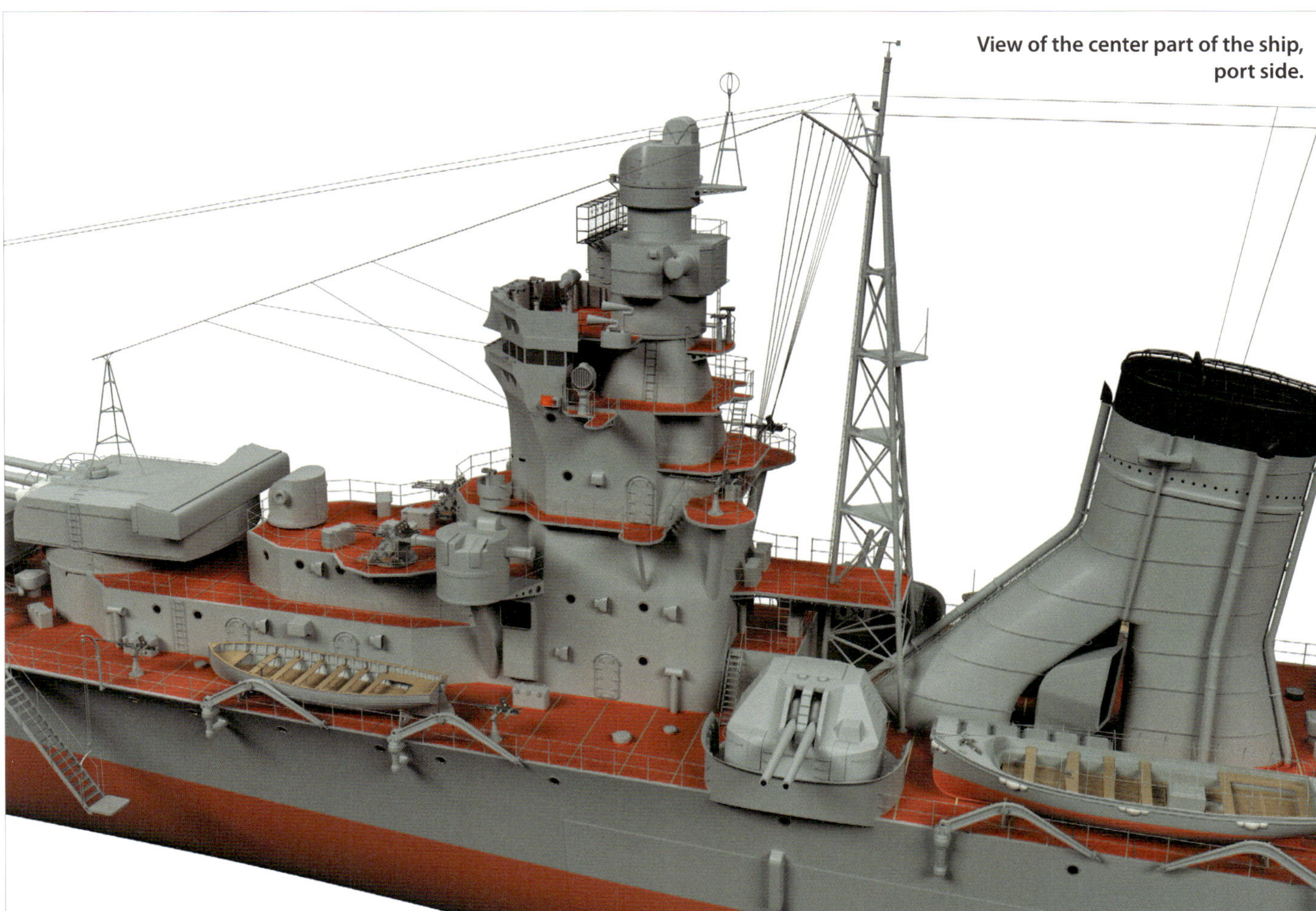

View of the center part of the ship, port side.

View of the center part of the ship, port side.

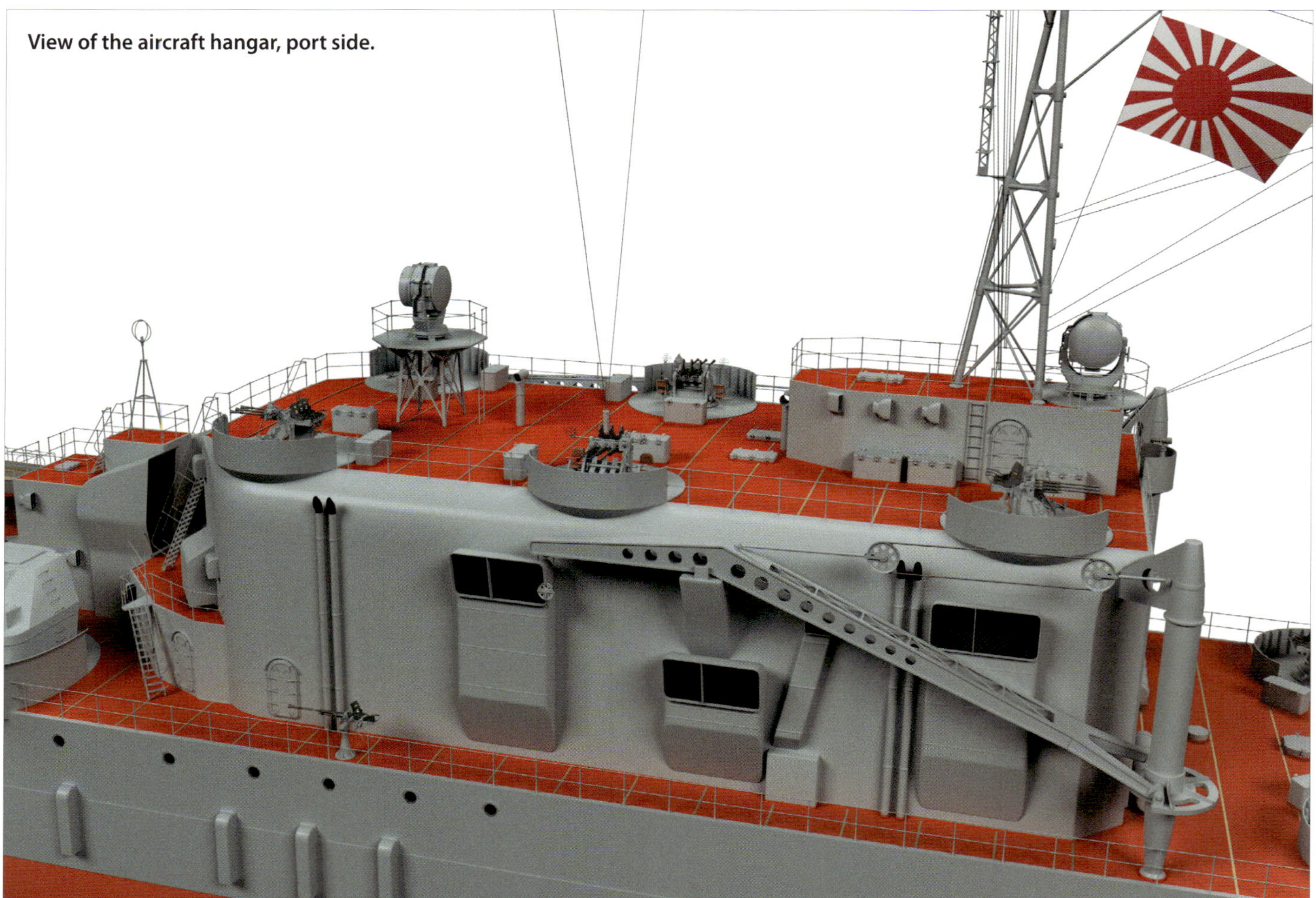

View of the aircraft hangar, port side.

View of the reconnaissance aircraft No. 1, port side.

View of the reconnaissance aircraft No. 2, port side.

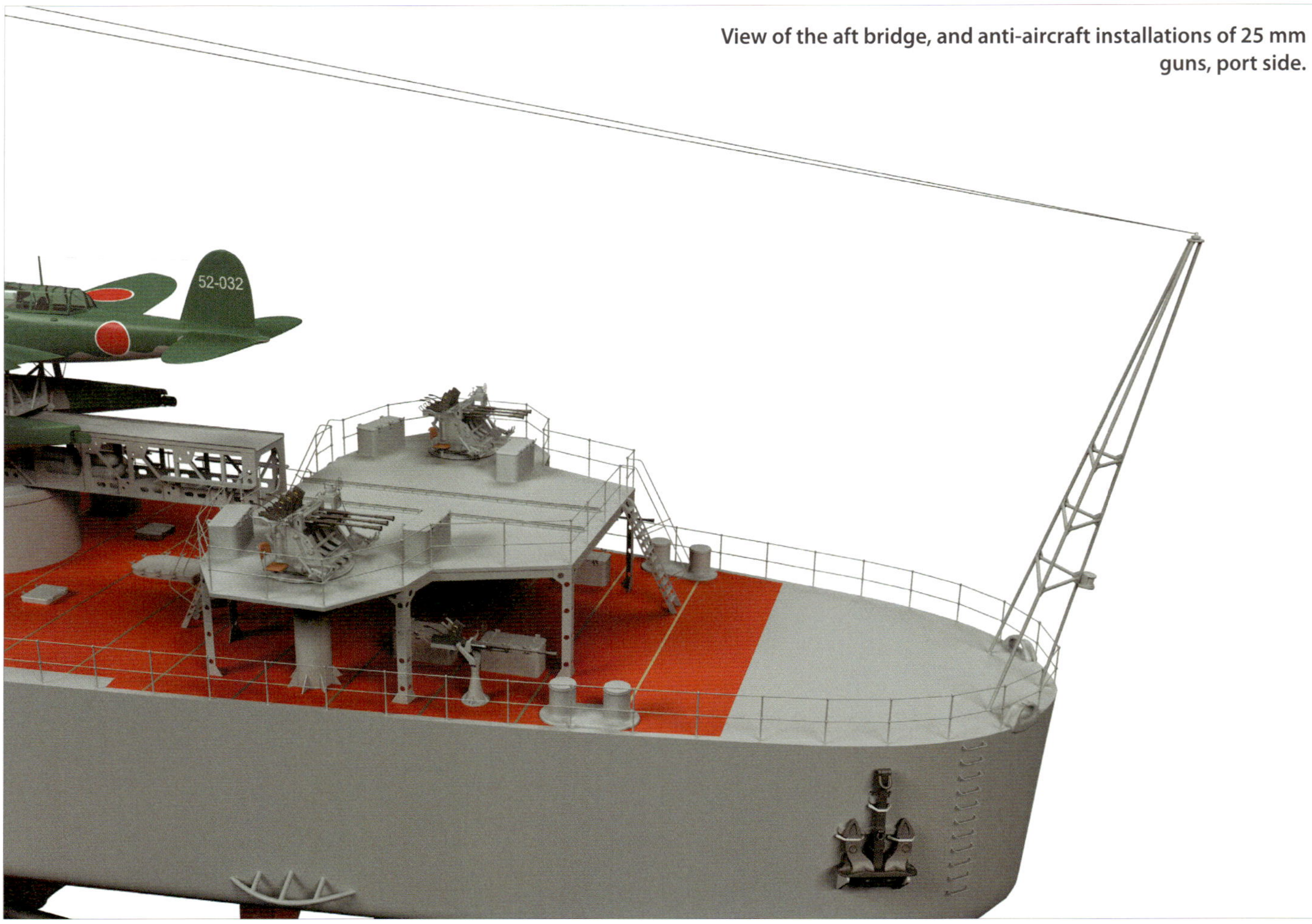

View of the aft bridge, and anti-aircraft installations of 25 mm guns, port side.

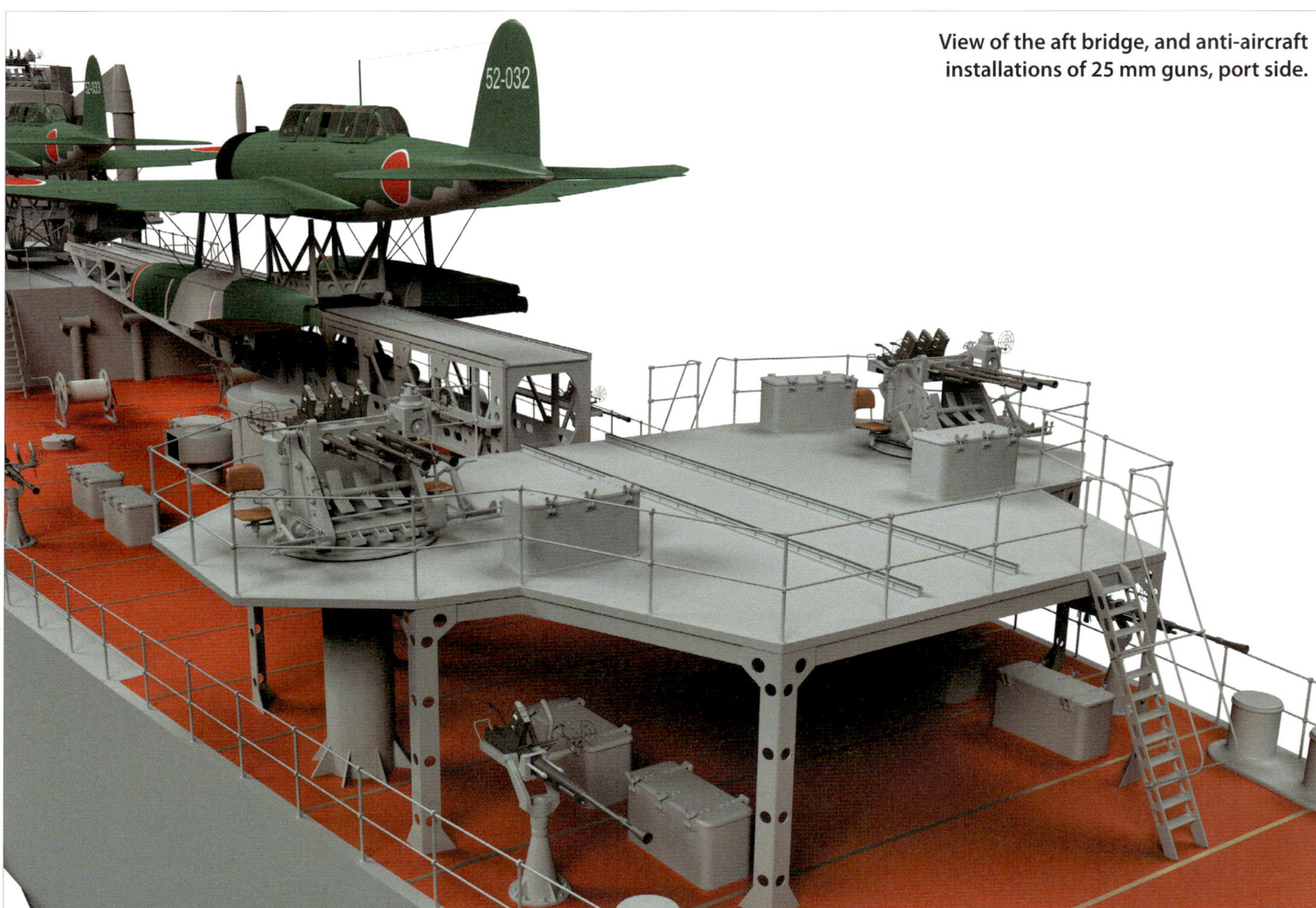

View of the aft bridge, and anti-aircraft installations of 25 mm guns, port side.

View of the aircraft hangar, port side.

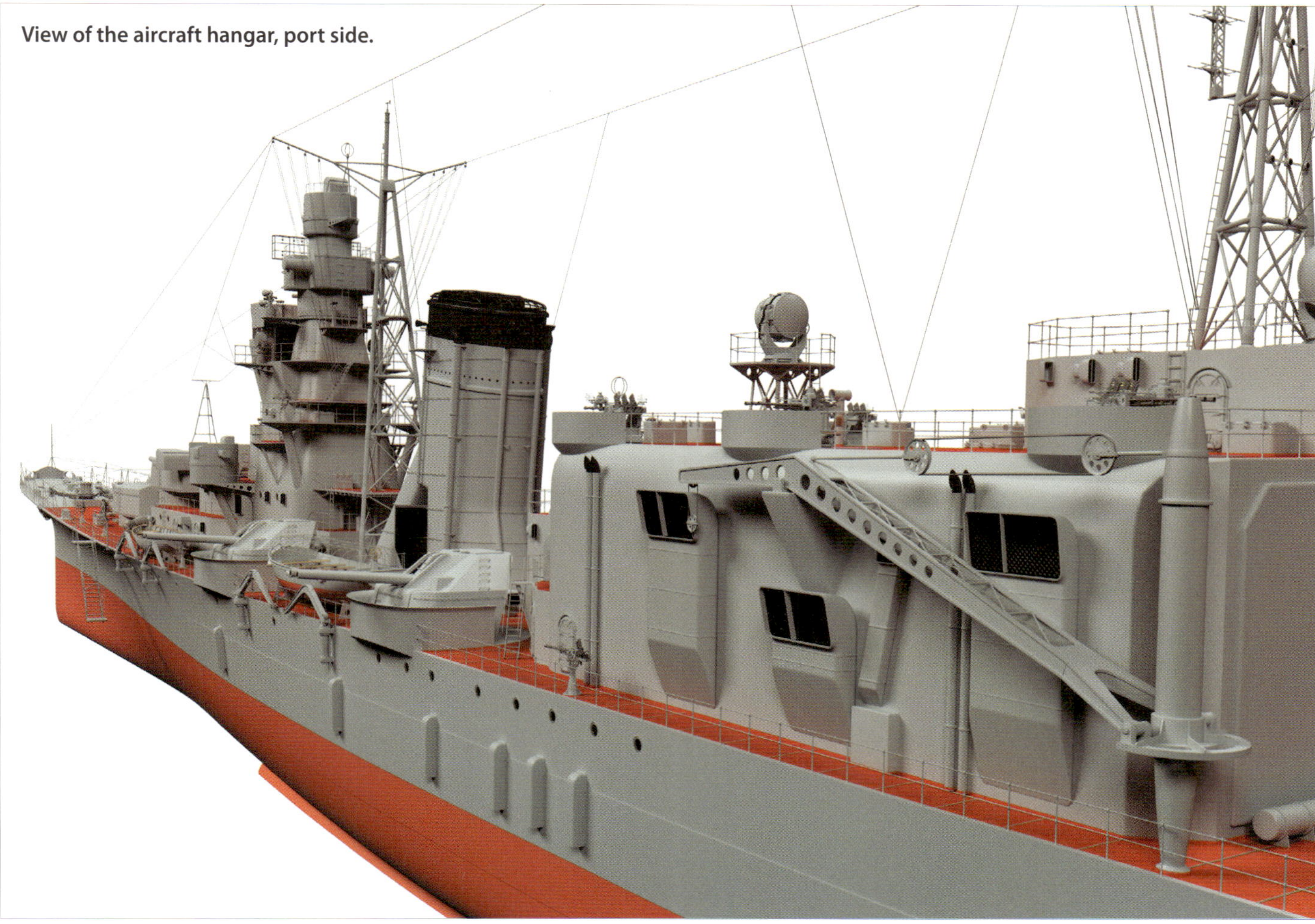

Overall view of the central part of the ship, port side.

Overall view of the central part of the ship, port side.

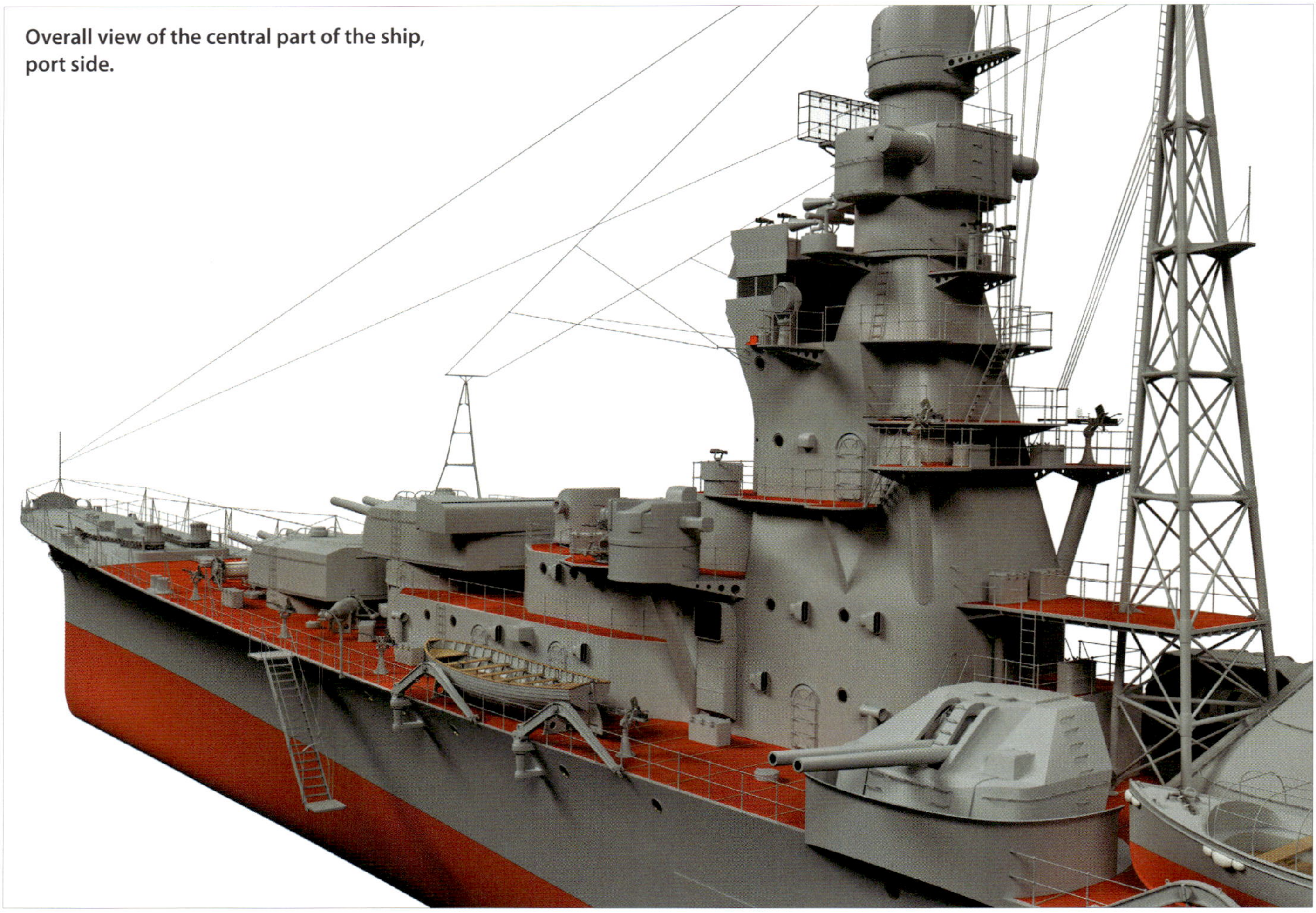

View of the bow, port side.

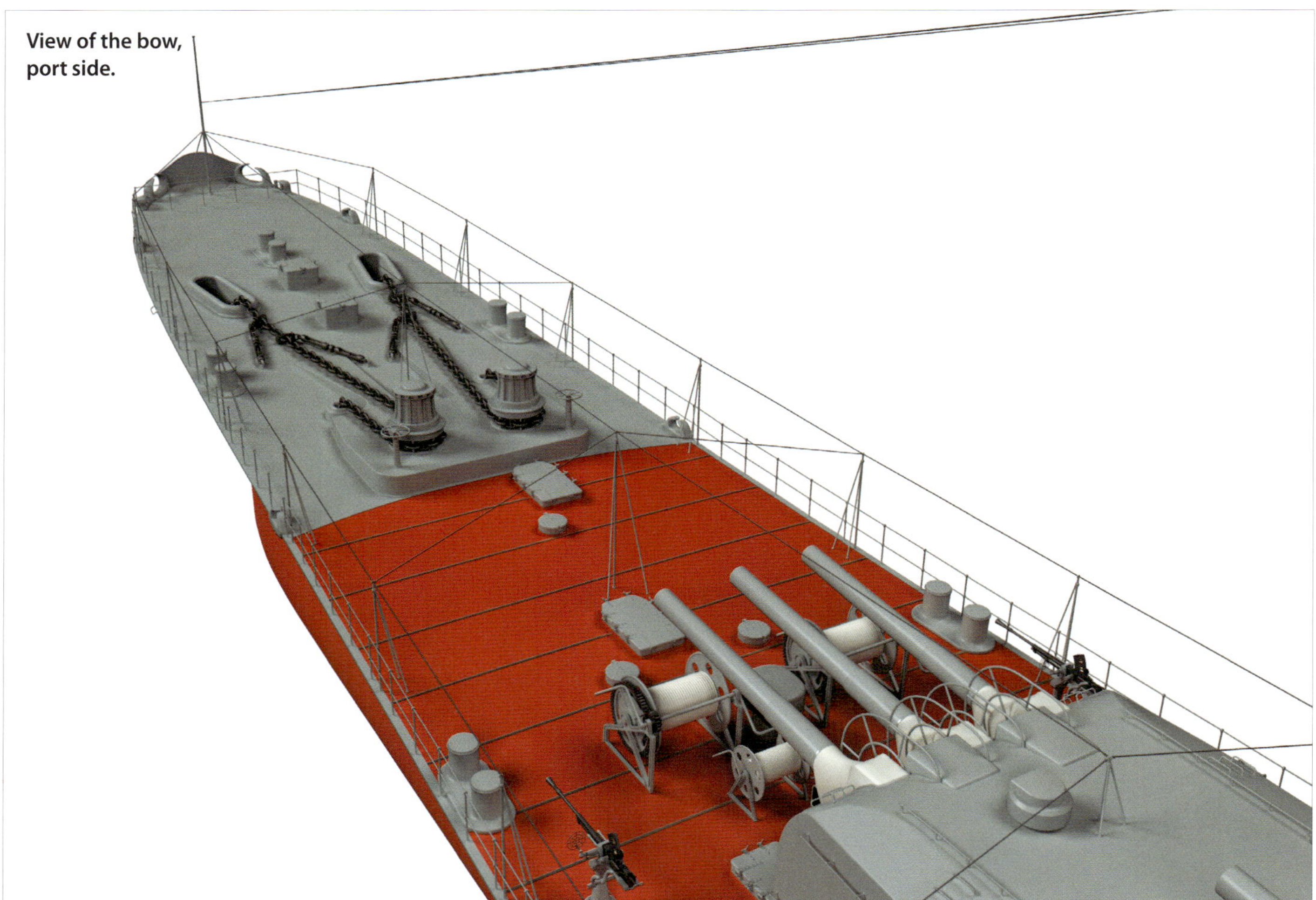

View of the turrets of 155mm guns, port side.

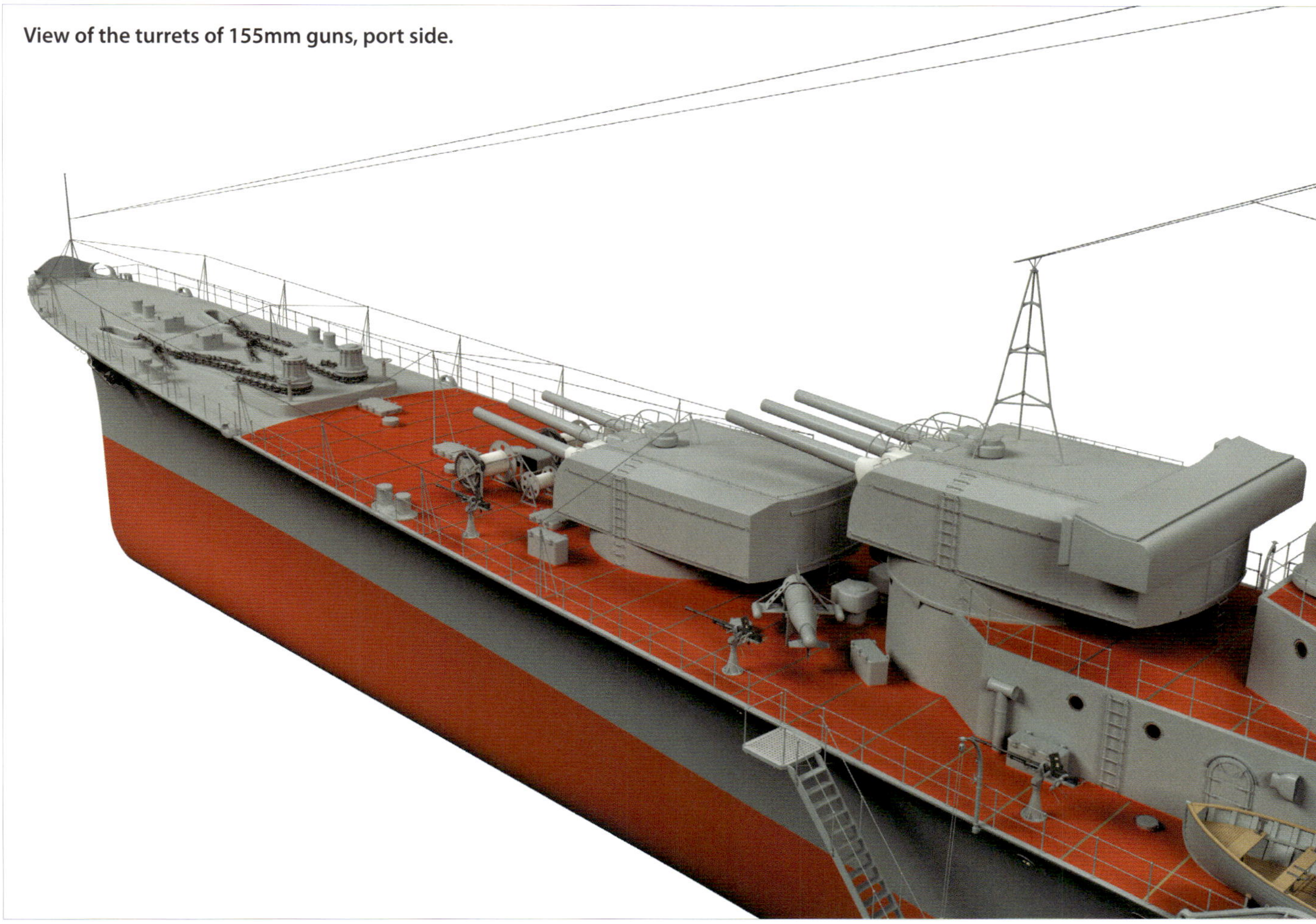

View of the forward superstructure of the ship, port side.

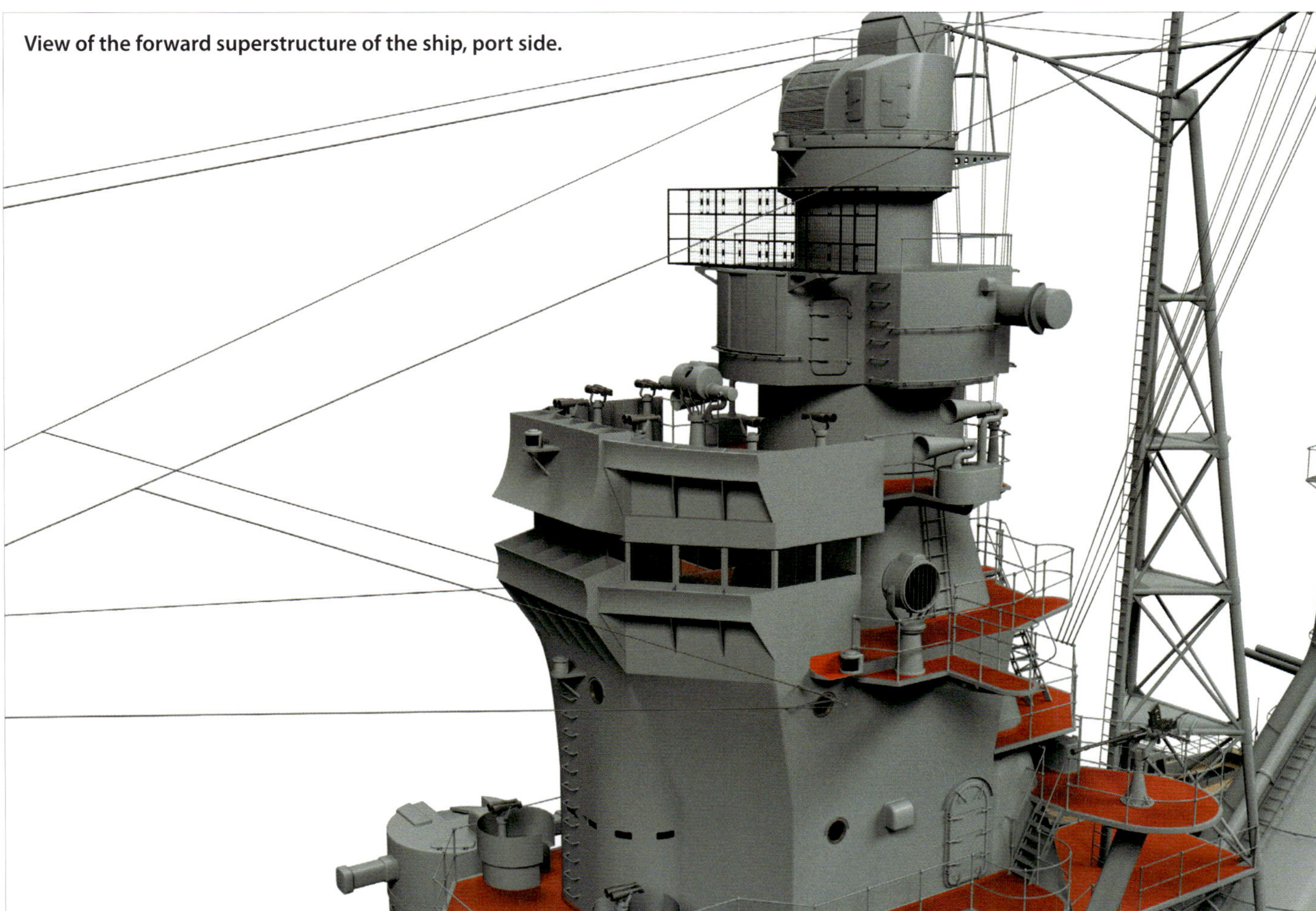

View of the turret "B" of 155mm guns, sport side.

View of the turrets of 155mm guns, port side.

View of the forward superstructure of the ship, port side.

View of the observation post, port side.

View of the turrets of 155mm guns.

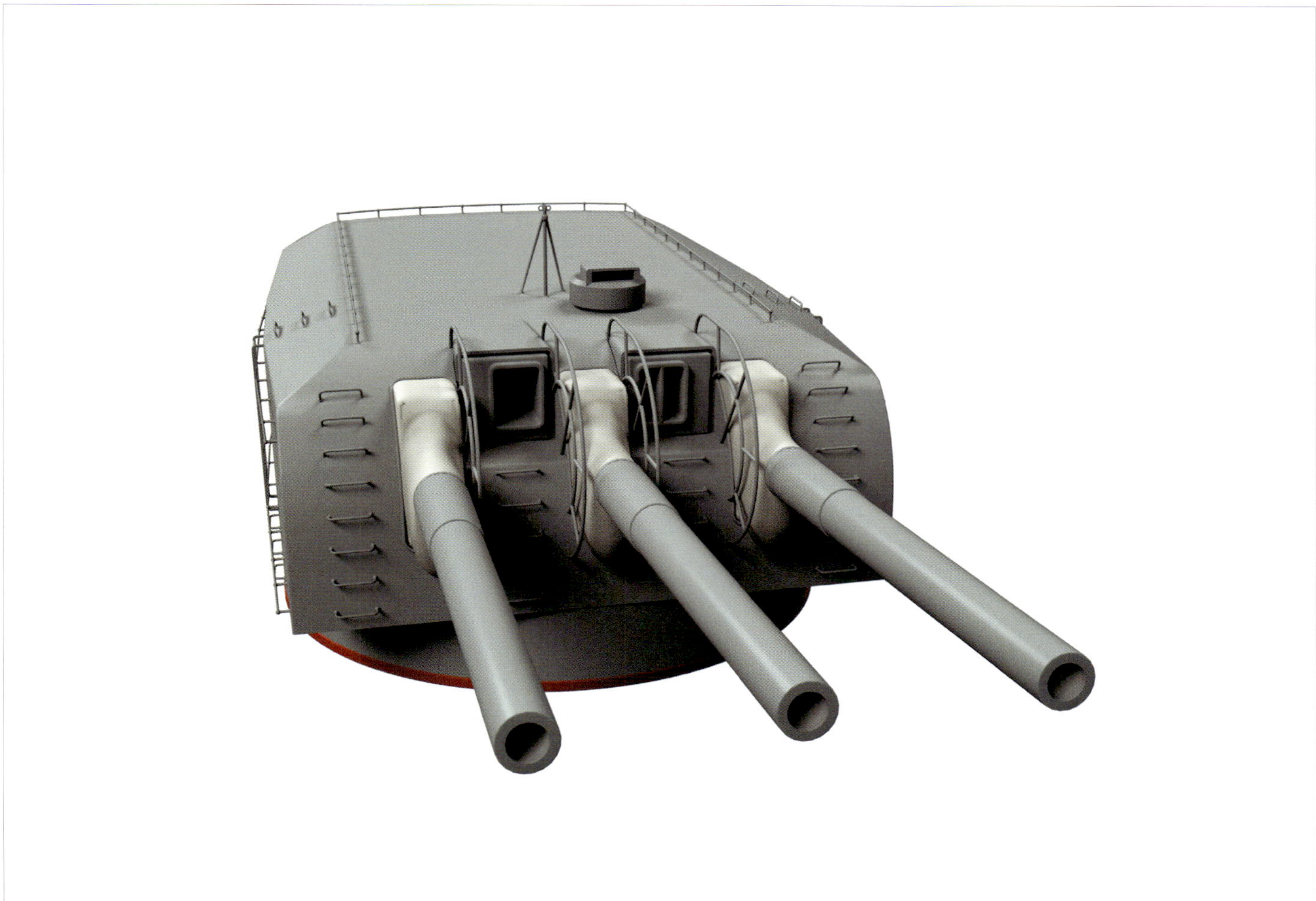

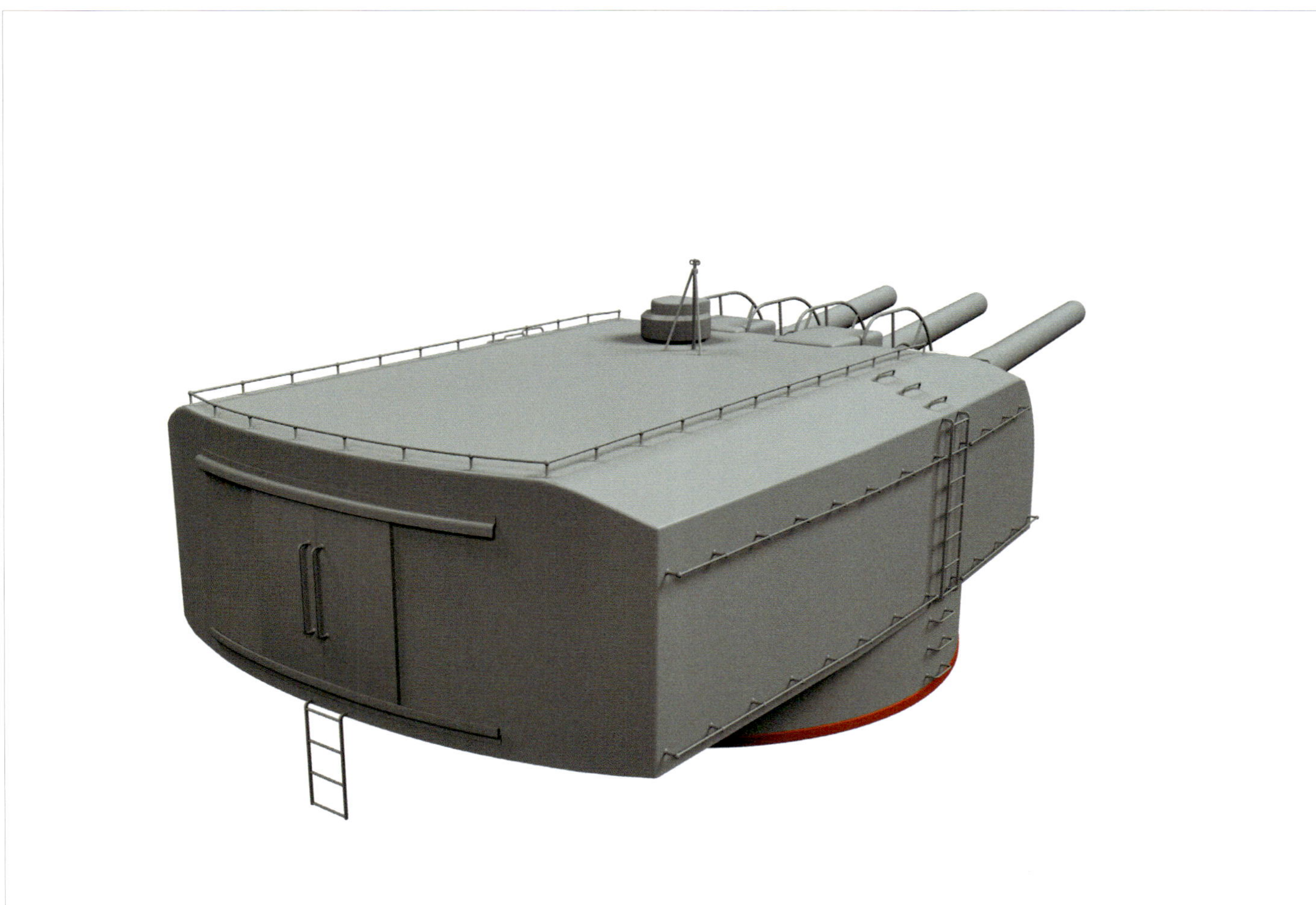

View of the turrets of 155mm guns.

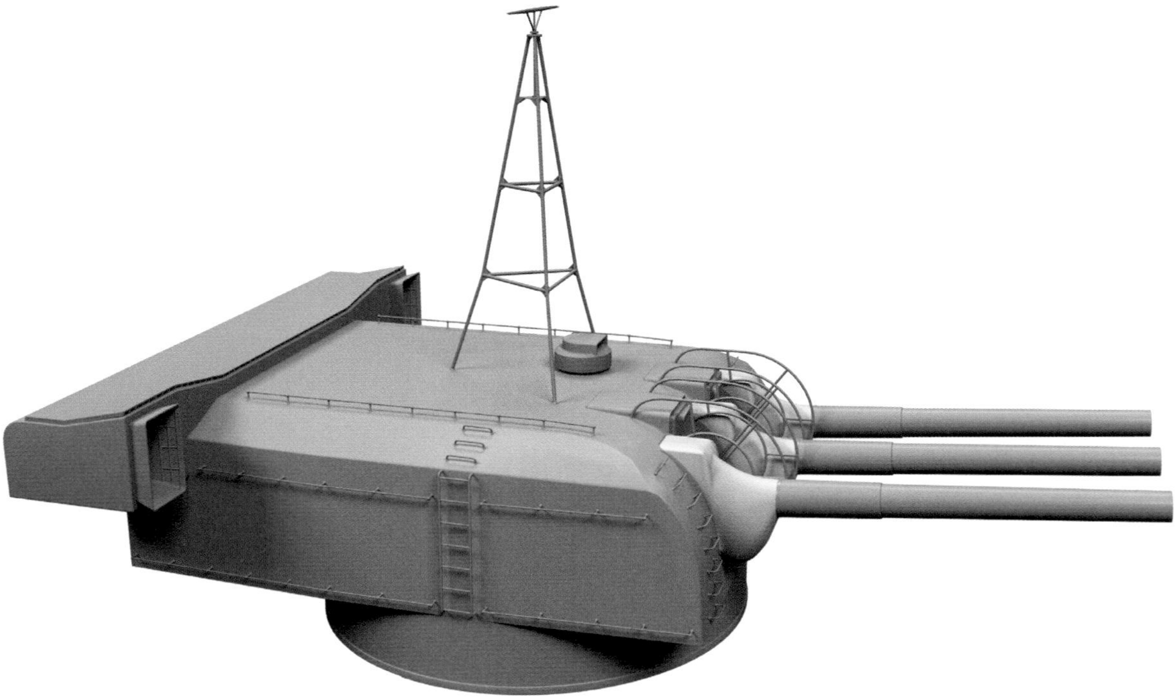

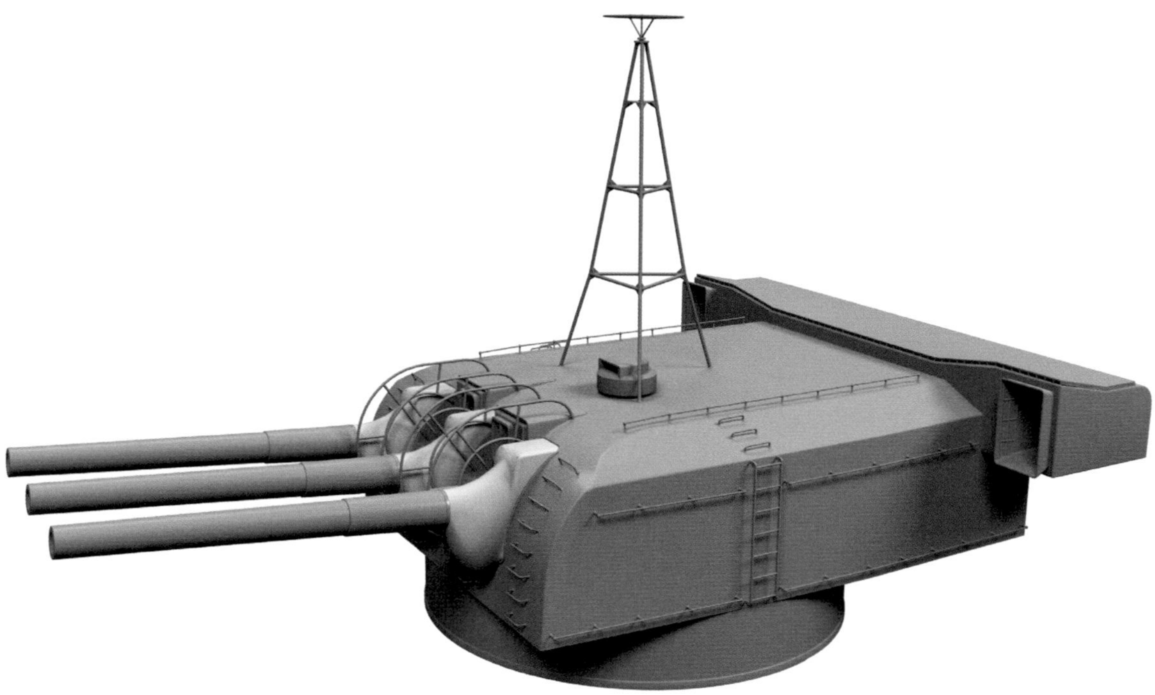

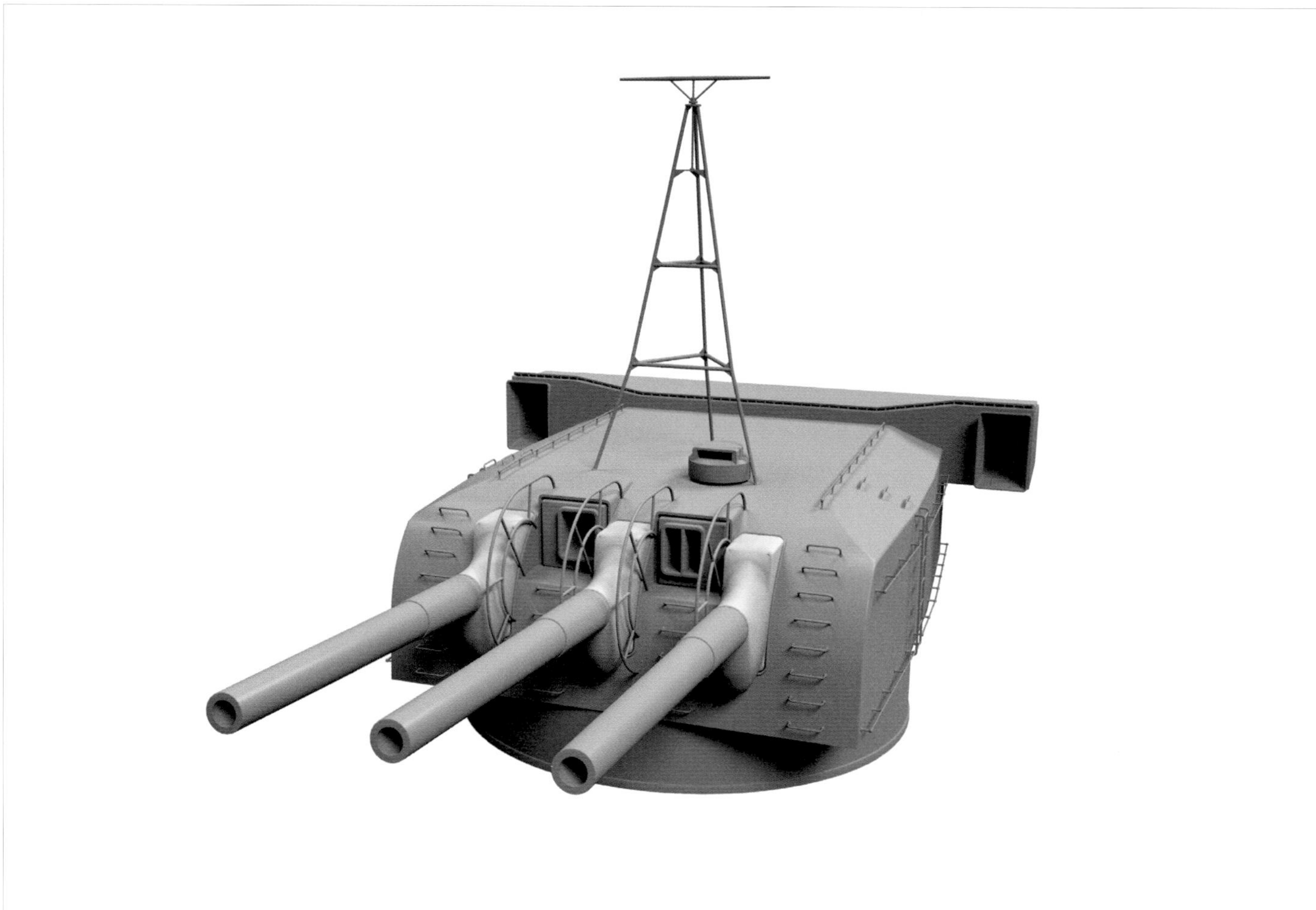

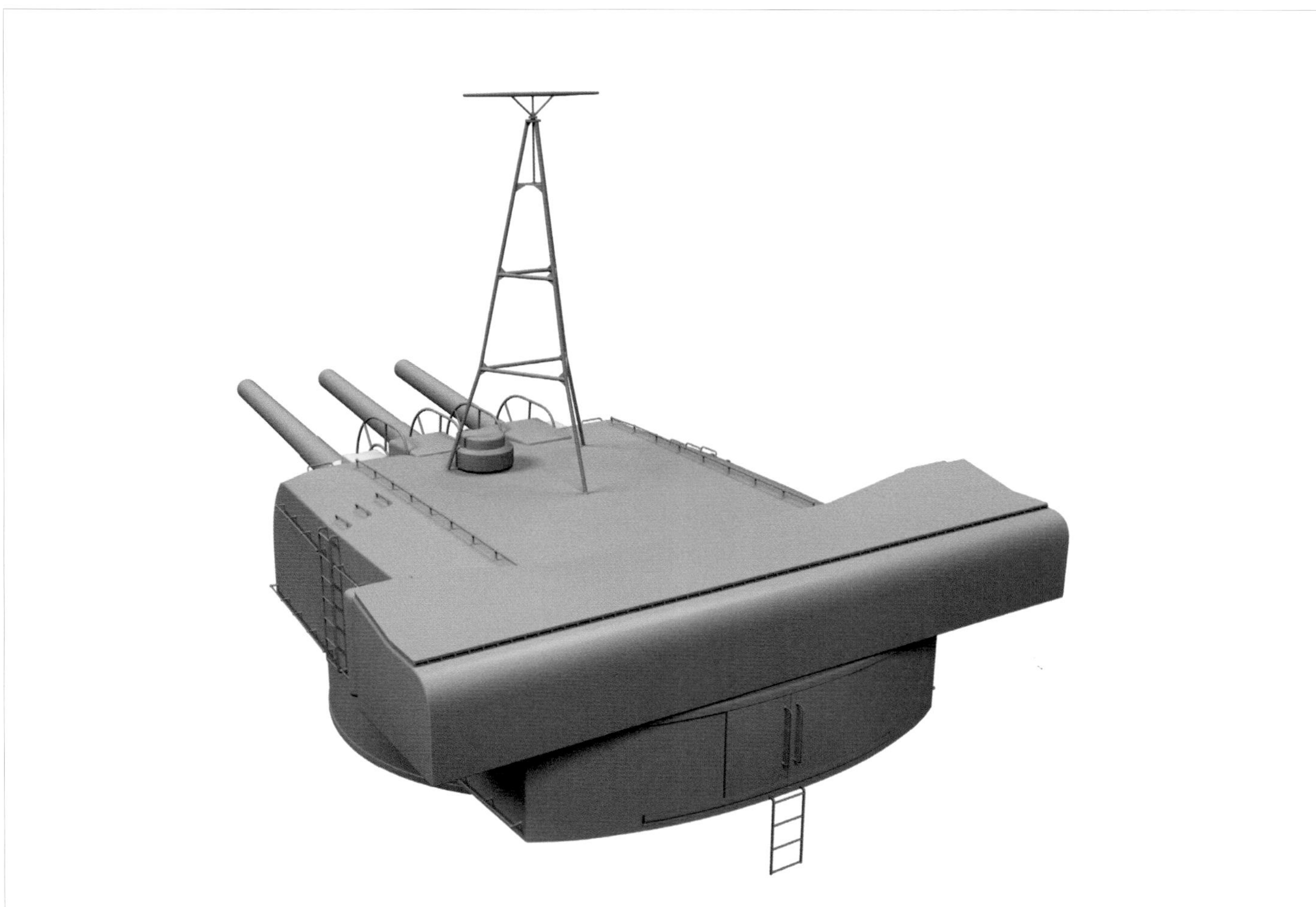

View of the universal installation of 100 mm guns.

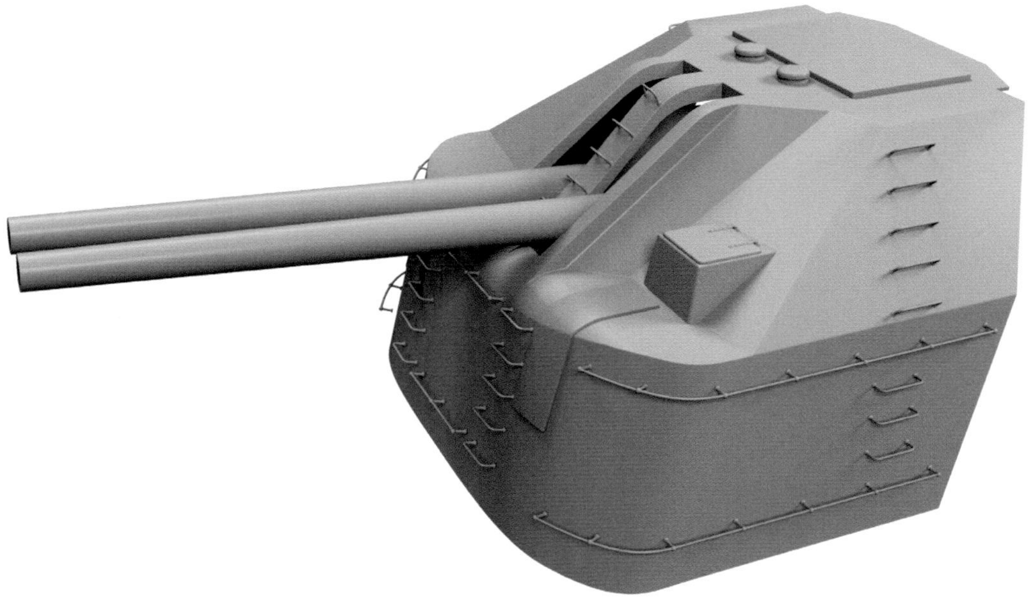

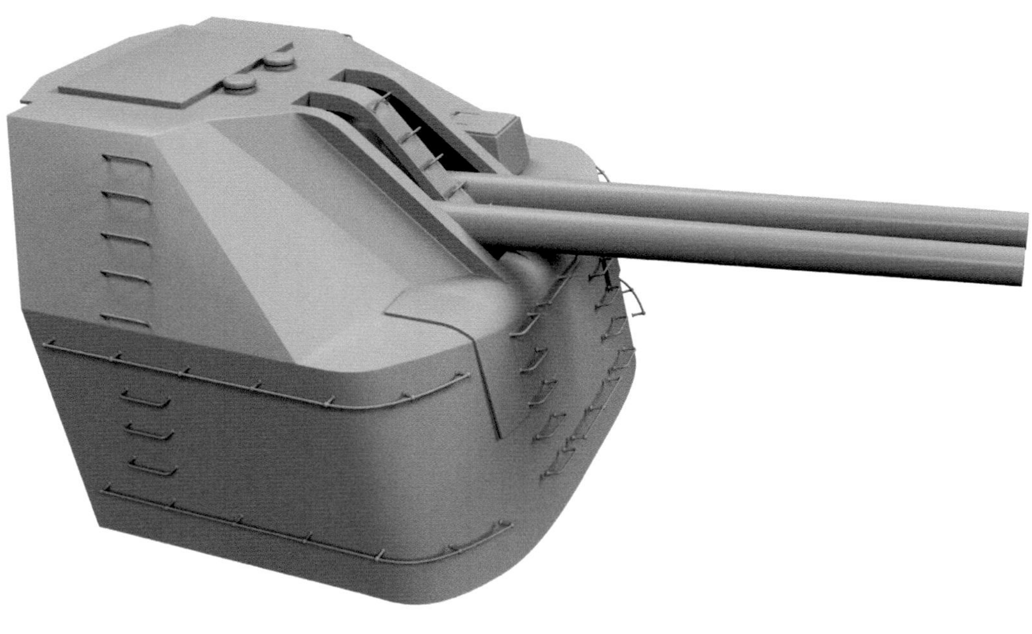

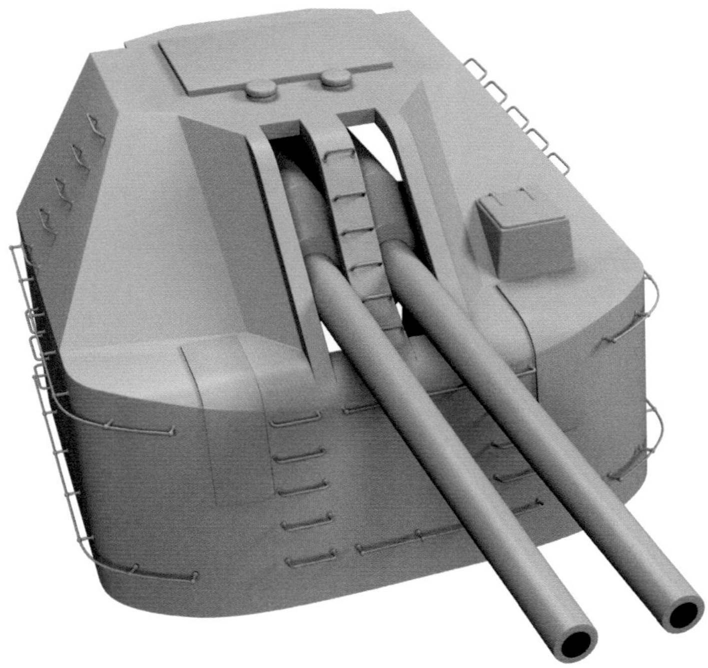

Type 96 25mm automatic cannon.

Type 96 triple AA 25mm automatic cannon.

Motor boat.

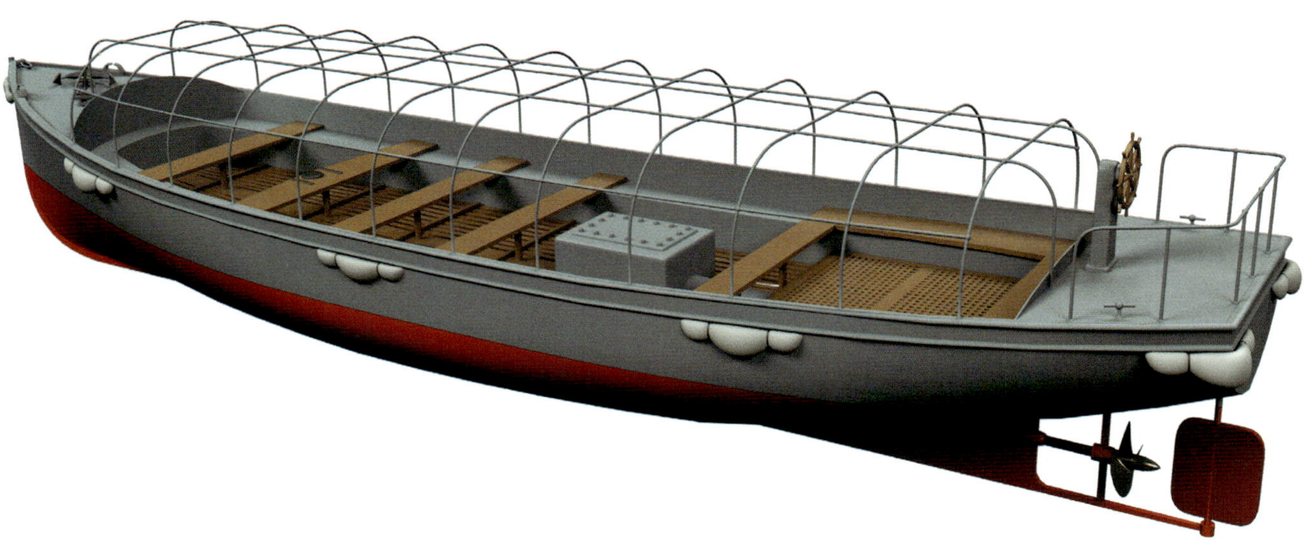

Motor boat.

Searchlight.

Catapult.

View of the reconnaissance aircraft on catapult.

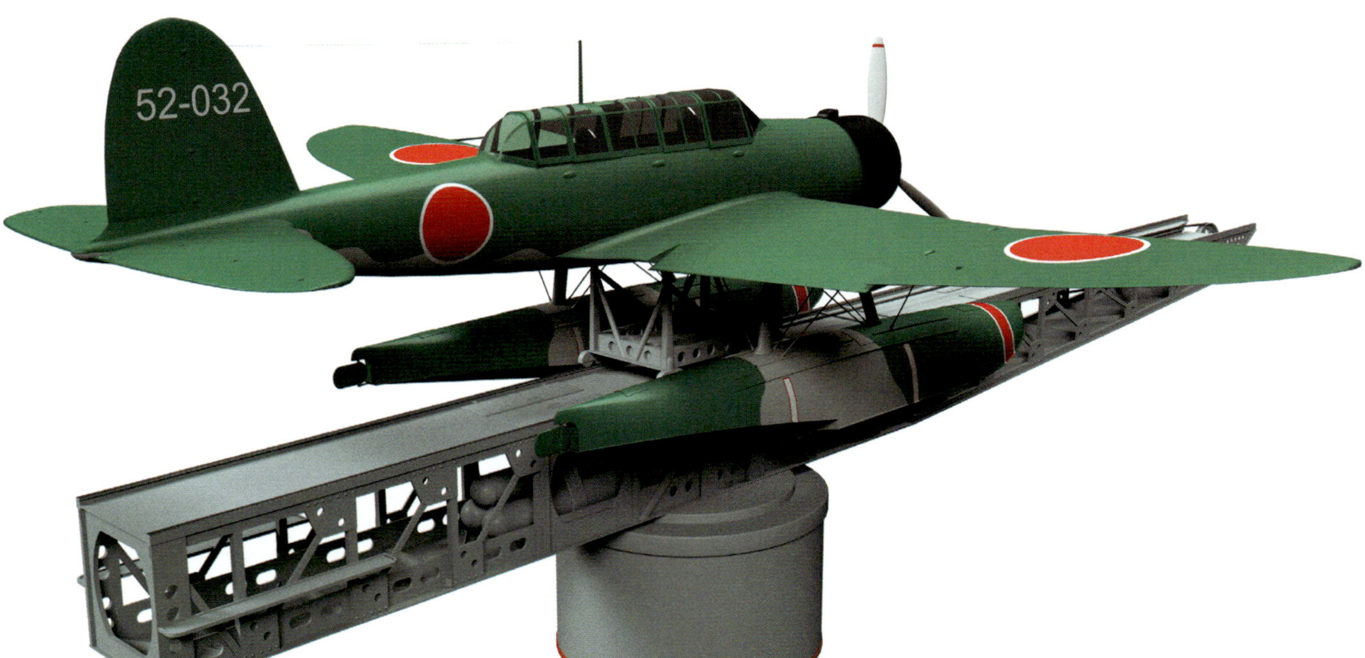

View of the reconnaissance aircraft.

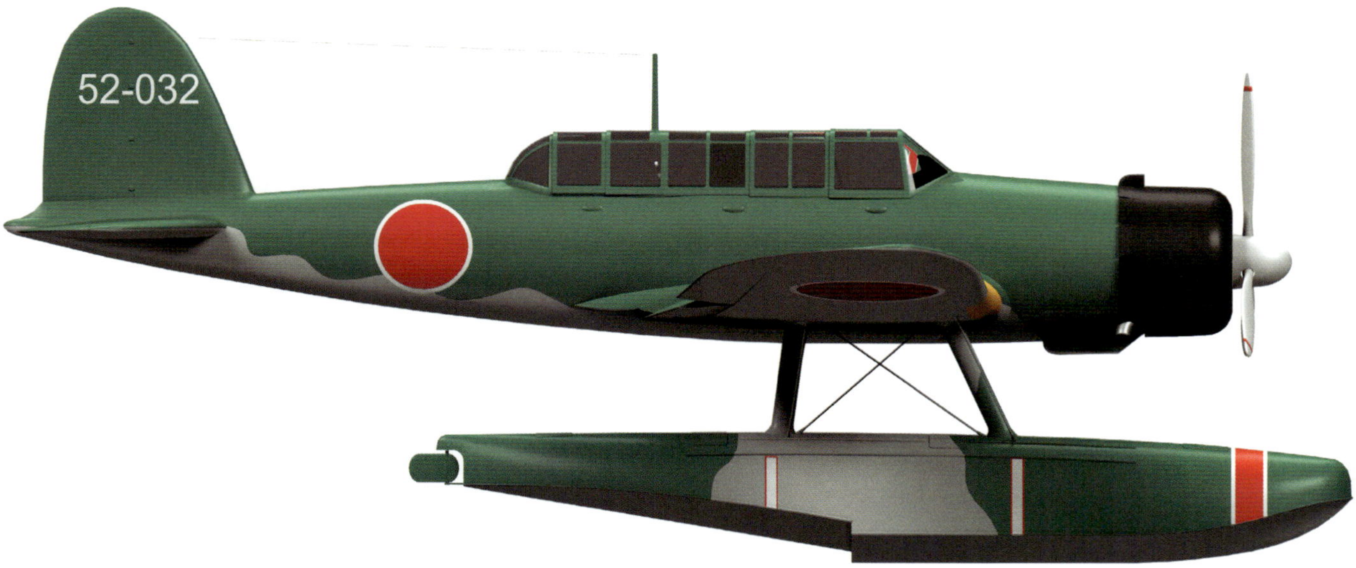

Overall view of the ship from the bow, starboard side.

Overall view of the ship from the bow, starboard side.

The Japanese Light Cruiser Ōyodo – Aliaksandr Sukhanevich

LUBLIN 2021 • ISBN 978-83-66673-65-6

3D illustrations and captions: **Aliaksandr Sukhanevich** • Text: **Jan Radziemski** • Text translation: **Stanisław Powała-Niedźwiecki** • Design: **KAGERO STUDIO** – Łukasz Maj

KAGERO Publishing • www.kagero.pl, e-mail: kagero@kagero.pl, marketing@kagero.pl

Editorial office, Marketing, Distribution: KAGERO Publishing, Akacjowa 100, os. Borek, Turka, 20-258 Lublin 62, Poland, phone/fax (+48) 81 501 21 05

w w w . k a g e r o . e u

3D visualisations are based on the available photographs, drawings and other archive data, and should be treated only as author's attempt to recreate the original look of the particular machine as faithfully as possible. If you are in possession of materials to which author did not reach, and you would like to help us to develop a better publication, please contact the Publisher on: redakcja@kagero.pl